Almost Nothing

Almost Nothing

Reclaiming Edith Farnsworth

NORA WENDL

3 FIELDS BOOKS
An imprint of the University of Illinois Press

3 Fields Books is an imprint of the University of Illinois Press.

Cataloging data available from the Library of Congress

ISBN 978-0-252-08876-6 (paperback)
ISBN 978-0-252-04797-8 (ebook)

This book is, in part, a memoir. Events are
described here as I experienced, interpreted, and
remember them. Although what is contained
in these pages is intended to evoke events of
the past, they cannot be perfectly re-created.

To live past the end of your myth is a perilous thing.

—*Anne Carson,* Red Doc>

1.

This is the history of a woman and her glass house. It is both of ours; it is hers and mine—a history of architecture, of women, and of glass. In short, it is a love story.

———

The house is a house, but it is also a metaphor; it has been described as a quantity of air trapped between a floor and a roof, as a threat to democracy, as a glass cage, and as a poem—all within the first few years of its existence. During its construction in rural Illinois from 1949 to 1951, it was believed by locals to be a tuberculosis sanitarium. It was met with confusion by the public. In 1953, a full two years after it was completed, *House Beautiful* took the position that Americans should be warned: it was a harbinger of imminent cultural dictatorship—*THE THREAT TO THE NEXT AMERICA.*

But the most popular metaphor is that this house is a lovechild, the result of an affair between the married architect Mies van der Rohe and his client Dr. Edith Farnsworth. Perhaps you know this; perhaps, like me, you are skeptical.

———

FIGURE 1. *Farnsworth House 8 Plano.*

You is complicated, Edith writes years after this house is completed. *You* could be any number of people. *You* could be the creature most adored. *You* may be some force of evil. And *you* may even become *I.*

———

If you ever decide to visit the house, you should go in the summer. The air will smell clean, with hints of recently clipped grass. You'll arrive at the edge of a gravel parking lot off Fox River Drive, where the visitor center sits, a simple, white, A-frame structure that evokes the strip mall buildings of the small midwestern towns nearby. Tucked behind a display of books is an improvised theater in which a thirty-minute documentary plays on a loop—the house is described here as *a one-of-a-kind glass house with a history of love affairs, lawsuits, and natural disasters.*

You may cringe at the moment in the documentary when the host turns theatrically to a woman who has written a play about this supposed love affair. *There's no tactful way to ask this question. Do you think they had a love affair?* he asks her in staged confidence. *Oh, I think so,* she responds. *What is more exciting than to have someone who is becoming world-renowned for his work, and he is interested in you? And you are making it possible for him to create something that has never been created before?* Posed at awkward angles around the bed at the east end of the glass house, they look at each other in silence, completely still in the moment after she speaks. This makes it seem as if there is some glitch in the film. The older couple in front of you will stand up and walk out, assuming this is the end of the story.

———

Edith. As I write, I have confusion over what to call her. When I write *her,* I will be speaking about Edith or other women I've known or been related to. They're all different people, but I can sense already a collapsing happening, like several panes of glass stacked against each other.

———

I can also tell you that what I sought was not always the truth—or that this was not the primary reason for my searching. That I did such strange things to feel close to her. That I waited for years to see this house, and that when I did finally visit it, I drove through the night across several state lines and arrived bleary-eyed through a gate in the chain-link fence surrounding it that was marked "Service Entrance." That it was a bleak midwestern February, the trees bare black lines against the empty, gray expanse of sky that drowned out even the sun. I couldn't hear myself think over the sound of ice-rain on the windshield. At a clearing, the caretaker's jeep—which had been leading me through the forest—slammed to a halt.

What I saw, I did not recognize as a house. It looked more like a land-locked ship: a rectangular glass box docked to what seemed to be a pier. A series of tall, slender I-beams painted an impossibly bright white rose from the earth to the full height of the house, a little more than fifteen feet. The glass box was pinned between these, its floor held five feet off the ground. Behind its glass walls, the curtains were drawn, cocooning it; the house seemed to be sleeping. I got out of the car to walk toward it, my shoes sinking into the earth—a reminder that this is a floodplain.

Inside, the caretaker asked me to remove my shoes and sign a waiver to acknowledge the rule against photographing the house from the interior while the curtains were closed. And so, I don't have a visual record, only the memory of it: the light that illuminated the curtains, that gave the house the feeling of an airplane rising through the fog. The caretaker jerked the curtains open with her bare hands, dragging them across the glass walls. Suddenly and without warning, the forest came sharply into view.

Glass may attempt invisibility, but it fails—always showing itself in a pale reflection or a streak of light. Glass does, though, render the world beyond it silent. I lay face down on the floor, felt the radiant heat against my whole body. On my belly, I began to photograph the house, to look for her here, to see where her feet would have met the ground. I only saw the thin steel legs of the furniture. I got up to discreetly photograph

FIGURE 2. *Edith Farnsworth House Terrace.*

the spaces I had promised not to photograph but found myself unable to resist. The caretaker stayed at the other end of the house, staring out a glass wall with her back to me—a silent contract between us as I documented the cracks in the plaster ceiling, bubbling paint that didn't quite conceal the rusting steel, the interior of a closet with a single tablecloth on a wire hanger, a cupboard full of more bottles of vodka than I could count.

In academia, you must commit yourself to a topic. You must lash yourself to it, they told me. But I found myself lashed to a ghost instead. There is no trace of her: the woman who commissioned this house, the woman who lived here. She moved into the house on December 31, 1950, and left it in the late 1960s; she has been gone for over fifty years. In her place, the house has been filled with furniture that the architect and his collaborator Lilly Reich designed for European houses and pavilions in the 1920s and 1930s—all of it made of steel and taut leather, the kind of furniture that repels human flesh and has to be sourced from museums and collectors, that comes with accession numbers, insurance, and handlers. It is by now a tourist destination, a piece of architectural history.

In her absence, I began to make a different kind of collection. It started small—I stole a blue scarf that I found in the courtyard of the apartment building where I lived at the time. I had seen my elderly neighbor wearing the scarf over her head, tied in a knot beneath her chin to protect her hair. It was thin and the most beautiful blue, oceanic. I could not bear to return it. It became a part of the Edith archive. Buckeyes my grandfather had given me for good luck. A pin from the Red Cross that I found in my grandmother's jewelry drawer. A few pink pieces of Depression glass. Old stamps. A small black, beaded purse my mother had given me. A Zeiss Ikon camera (nonfunctioning). White saucers and coffee cups. Anything that I encountered, anywhere, that I believed she would have used or touched.

When I exhibited these objects publicly, I said they were her things. I said it without hesitation. I said it because I stole them, found them, procured them, organized them as if I were her.

It felt like a way of writing her back into existence. It felt like revenge against the first historian of the house, Franz Schulze, who had described her as *equine in feature*. Although she was a renowned physician and researcher—finding a cure for nephritis, a once-fatal kidney disease—and although she commissioned one of the most remarkable houses in the world from one of the most famous architects—the first woman in the United States to build and then live in an experimental glass house—she appears in history for the first time in a biography of the architect, described as his former (and jilted) lover.

It is the only place in architectural history where a woman's body is given such considerable study: she is described as *six feet tall and ungainly of carriage*. The architect's attempts to sue her for ownership of the house and to displace her from it as soon as it was complete are dismissed as a mere *rupture*, romanticized as *a breakup*. This history is written after both the architect and doctor have died, the historian turning to their family members, friends, and colleagues to reconstruct their relationship. Schulze even interviews her estranged sister, Marion, who says Edith was mesmerized by the architect. Schulze cites the architect himself as exclaiming that *the lady expected the architect to go along with the house*, but there is nothing to indicate when and where he made this statement, nothing to ground it.

And so, it is taken for granted that they were lovers.

And I became curious about what that might mean, what difference it might make to a building, how we cannot imagine a history of architecture in which men and their erections are not central; how to write a history of architecture in which men and their erections are peripheral, or rather, to see if I can imagine one.

2.

There should be a word for one person's gravitational pull on another, how gravity isn't linear but is what happens when a person falls into the fold that another person creates in space. I fall into the space around her, and I begin to orbit.

I have read all of the theories about how the architect and the client entered each other's orbit, but the one that is most outstanding is the idea that she conspired it: that she had mutual friends throw a dinner party to which she and the architect would be invited and that she planned to ask him to design her a house. In other words, another woman setting yet another trap. Most historians say that he stunned her with his brilliance, arguing that in her memoirs she recorded his presence as *tremendous, like a storm, a flood*.

But I have read all of her unpublished memoirs, and I enjoy knowing that she found his silence puzzling, that she and her companions chatted around his granite form as he ate, ignoring them, until he finally broke his sullen silence by saying he would love to design a house for her. She sarcastically registers his announcement as being like an *act of God.*

———

When I began my academic career, I was handed a curriculum inherited from men riffing on the ideas of the man who built this glass house. Everything was abstract, not actual. One of my colleagues had convinced the students that when distant things aligned in space—say, the edge of a house and the edge of the detached garage behind it—it was because actual, invisible lines called *regulating lines* magnetically drew them together. The students' writing assignments were peppered with imaginary lines between things. *I saw the regulating lines extending from the edges of the building as I approached it.* I took the students into the school's large atrium and I asked them to kick all the regulating lines.

Just because we can't kick it doesn't mean it's not there, said one of the students. *I can't kick gravity.*

Instead of arguing, I found theories to support this idea. There are invisible forces that tether buildings in place: longing, money, desire, and politics. What Jennifer Bloomer writes—*for a nexus of lines, whether drawn, virtual, stimulated, or troped, is the mark of a longed-for object.*

I sat in my office searching the internet for images with such lines. I read once that in the early days of perspective drawing, the vanishing point—the convergence of these invisible lines—would be concealed by a painted panel and a golden lock, because to look at the vanishing point, even the humanly constructed one, would be to try to look God square in the eye. I search for the source of this information, cannot find it, and begin to wonder if I invented it. Instead, every history of perspective drawing seems to begin with an Albrecht Dürer print from 1600. It shows a draughtsman at his drawing table: a naked woman reclines on this table, revealing her vagina. He frowns as he peers at it through a pane of glass that is inscribed with a grid. He is trying to draw what he sees, this dark and hairy abyss, but he is never even able to put down the first line.

———

The architect read Catholic philosophers Saint Augustine, Saint Thomas Aquinas, and Romano Guardini. Always audible behind Guardini, experts note, is Nietzsche, famous for writing *God is dead. God remains dead. And we have killed him.* There is some evidence, though, that the architect may

The National Book Critics Circle Biography Award 2025

have thought of architecture as a place to receive a message from God, from the beyond, from the distance, from the vanishing point, that infinite that is a speck, a nothing. There is, of course, no mention of what this message is.

Almost nothing, *beinahe nichts*, was his concept for her glass house. Almost what—almost God? I wonder whether the nothingness he subscribed to was one she would even recognize.

Sometimes the *almost nothing* can knock us down. Online, I find a video of a woman in a long dress who keeps tripping over a lawn chair that she approaches on a windy, grassy hill. She manages to sit in it and then falls, tipping out on purpose. This is an homage to the work of Dutch artist Bas Jan Ader, who was obsessed with handing himself over to gravity. He had started by merely flinging himself off a roof, then a tree. He tumbled, headlong, into bushes. He filmed all of it. In some of these films, he has a difficult time submitting to this invisible force. In *Broken Fall (Geometric)* (1971) he tries to fall over a metal stand—he starts to tip, but his right leg catches him. Start, catch. The body cannot simply let itself fall over. In another attempt, on another day, he succeeds: he rolls down the roof of his family home and into some bushes.

Gravity made itself master over me, he writes.

When the woman in the video extends her hands to break her fall, I want to say to her, *You're weak, too.*

———

My teaching fellowship is ending. When the letter comes from the prestigious university telling me that I've been accepted into a competitive postgraduate program, I am astonished. It is precisely the world I desire and can't pay for. I take the tenure-track job I am offered instead.

———

I try the tumbling game on my drive across the country, from my visiting faculty position in North Carolina to a tenure-track position in Oregon. In Saint Louis, I stop at an overgrown plot of land where, in 1972, the thirty-three towers of the Pruitt-Igoe housing complex, among the first racially integrated public housing projects in the United States, were dynamited. After standing a mere eighteen years, explosives were packed deep into the towers' foundations: the housing authority did not properly maintain the towers but instead blamed the tenants, largely working class and Black, for faulty plumbing, burst pipes, malfunctioning electricity, and cheap hardware that fell apart upon use. They then dramatically destroyed the evidence of their own failure. The towers fell like curtains, and their rubble still occupies the site. I make my way through the broken fence surrounding it and to the center of it all, an accidental, overgrown forest that conceals this history. I set up a tripod. Then I try and try to make myself fall to the ground like one of these towers without catching myself. Each time, I drop to my knees.

What is this internal mechanism that saves us from falling?

I Google *Why can't we make ourselves fall over*, and the search returns: *12 answers: Why can't we make ourselves fall in love?*

————

The architect trusts the doctor enough to ask her to write an essay about his work not long after they meet. And yet, in the essay, she barely mentions his work.

The essay is not signed, so when I find it by accident in the Ryerson & Burnham Libraries at the Art Institute of Chicago, where I stop during my drive west to Oregon, it seems at first like an anonymous essay. The first page of it is marked with rust in the shape of a paperclip at the top left, and it is attached to a draft of an essay by James Speyer that was later published in *Art Papers*. Edith's essay has only existed in rumor before, and yet I hold it in my hands. I know it is hers because she has left me a crumb, the use of the word *sequela*, a medical term referring to an aftereffect of a disease—an unexpected result or complication. As in, for the architect, *structure was the sequela of the material . . . structure was good when it conformed to the nature of the material.*

After I get my Xerox of it, I leave the dark library and its hushed tones to sit in my car in a nearby parking deck and circle her words. I am trying to land on the things that drew her to him.

She devotes less time to describing his architecture and more to describing what is beyond it.

She writes that his buildings are not buildings but solutions to the human experience. They are not products of this earth but products of an imagination; that imagination is not working to express itself but to resolve *the perception of underlying relations* between *space and line*, between *thought and feeling.*

I have to remind myself that the architect's most famous buildings are glass towers that were never actually built. His Friedrichstrasse skyscraper project of 1921, a drawing comprised of a series of vertical lines framing blank, reflective glass walls that seem to have erupted from the dark street below. With heavy, black charcoal, he managed to draw what the eye perceives to be glass.

She explains the human imagination as a rocket that *can only fly upwards in the dark universe and rapidly expend its energy, not to be followed or profited by, but only imitated and exaggerated.*

Because it burns out.

There is a vanishing point in her essay, a paragraph that drifts off into nothing, a half sentence: she describes the architect in his formative years, developing his eye by searching through the ancient dwellings and buildings of   . She does not know where, and perhaps where doesn't matter. Maybe she intended to fill it in later. Maybe she asked him, and he didn't respond. Or maybe   is the place.

I put down the essay and drag an envelope out of my glove compartment. When I left North Carolina, I received a going-away present from a colleague, an envelope full of his favorite sentences from his favorite books. The first one that I pull out reads:

If she had a religion, it was biological.

I tape it to my steering wheel.

It reminds me that in July 1975, Bas Jan Ader took to the sea in the smallest sailboat ever to cross the Atlantic: he called it the *Ocean Wave*. After years of submitting himself to gravity on land, he would submit himself to the ocean, where the moon's gravity pulls the ocean water outward, and the earth spins, pulling ocean water inward: he would give his body over to this conflict, a gravity larger than his resistance. He called this project *In Search of the Miraculous.*

———

When I stop at the glass house in Plano, Illinois, for yet another tour, I tell the tour guide that I am curious about Edith's memoirs, and she tells me that *everything that woman wrote is a lie.* I ask her what else history is made of, and she slams the golf cart to a stop, bruising my knees on the dashboard.

———

Gravity won: Bas Jan Ader's boat was found empty off the coast of Ireland.

———

I keep driving west, knees throbbing.

What Baudrillard asks and immediately answers: *Is it normal to build and construct? No, it is not.*

When we build, we are building a space for something that does not yet exist in the world. And yet, things are destroyed all the time that must be replaced: a building slowly burning to the ground, the people driving by who have stopped to watch the tongues of flame, to smell the heat.

This is the last thing she records seeing on her drive west to the land on which she wants to build her house. It is 1943, maybe 1944. Recently, the Society Section of the *Chicago Tribune* has observed that her graduation from medical school is a *curious thing*, that she has *burst the bonds of social life*. It is noted that *now that her associate, Lieut. Col. Herbert Barker, is off on military service with the Passavant hospital unit in February, [she] finds herself with added responsibility.*

It concludes with a pivot: *Miss Farnsworth is a tall, handsome girl with a splendid physique and much enthusiasm for her chosen avocation.* In 1942, when this is printed, she is thirty-eight years old.

She passes fields of soybeans, corn, animals, experimental farms, a reminder that when half the world is away at war, the other half must stay and cultivate, must lay low and learn to remake the world from nothing, with nothing.

There is a way in which a road changes what is aimless into meaning—a decision to turn left after the railroad becomes a slow descent, becomes parking the car, becomes walking through a fallow field, becomes removing her shoes, pulling her skirt around her waist and wading into the river, turning her back to the bridge behind her and feeling the river stream between her legs, knowing that falling back would set her afloat perhaps for miles, even in the slow-turning Fox River.

She began negotiating for this nine-acre strip of land with Colonel McCormick, owner of the *Chicago Tribune*. On the deed, drawn up in 1945, she is recognized as Edith Farnsworth (Unmarried Woman).

3.

The architect suggests making her house out of glass on his very first visit to the river with her. Glass is something, but it is barely something—a whisper of a barrier, two thin lines traced on paper. When she asks, *why glass*, he acts as if this is obvious, and she nods *of course*, and the surface of the river rolls, trying to tell her something.

———

A friend and I rent hundreds of dollars of scaffolding and a truck to drive it to my studio apartment. Together, we move all of my belongings into the hallway. We are in my apartment constructing a functionless space out of this emptiness, *to serve for nothing, relate to nothing*, in the words of Georges Perec. Slowly, over the course of the day, building with our hands, like animals, we erect a perfect and structurally sound ten-foot cube in the center of my apartment and shroud it in dusty black construction fabric that we cut to be perfectly taut, even though it is also rented and cutting it is destroying it, and destroying what you have rented means owning it (for a price far greater than it is worth). Neighbors returning home from work stop by to admire it—a huge black cube in the center of my apartment, useless for anything but forcing me to slide along the wall to reach the sink, or the windows, or the tiny hallway leading to the tiniest bathroom. Useless for anything but perpetual motion; the space it creates is the space of one person orbiting nothing.

A space, I repeat, that would serve no purpose at all, writes Perec.

———

FIGURE 3. Ludwig Mies van der Rohe, Farnsworth House, Plano, Illinois, 1945.

The architect made the first drawing of this house right after his site visit. It is a watercolor of a glass box floating in the air. There are solid boxes inside the glass box and you can see through the glass to the trees beyond. They have a canopy but no trunks: these trees do not touch the earth. The solid boxes and what they hold are mysteries.

————

I think about the research I could do without having to check my body at the door. I need to be closer to the glass house, closer to the history that I am studying, that I am trying to write in my own particular way. I tell a colleague this.

What, he asks, *are you a method historian now?*

Apparently so.

Before I leave, I begin collecting quotes about the house from experts. Max Protetch, a curator familiar with the house, says, *It is helpful if you think of this house as if it were a beautiful human being. Think of it as if falling in love with someone who gives you nothing back.*

————

I move to Chicago with these questions. She was a brilliant woman. Did she accept his strange proposal, a glass house, because of her desire for him or because of her desire for the unknown? I already know it was for the unknown, but I feel the need to prove it. Did she think of him as a genius? Did she think of herself that way?

What is genius? *Some people,* Derrida writes, *would say that* genius *amounts to a one-person genre.* This is just another way of saying that genius surpasses all that is general: surpasses genre, gender, sexuality. But it goes further than this: *each time that one allows oneself to say "genius," one suspects that some superhuman, inhuman, even monstrous force comes to exceed or overturn the order of species of the laws that govern genre.*

Why do we desire people we perceive to be *genius*?

For professor and writer Jane Gallop, it was *to make them more human, more vulnerable.* She speaks of her two professors, two men she slept with during graduate school. *These two had enormous power over me: I don't mean their institutional position, but their intellectual force. I was bowled over by their brilliance; they seemed so superior. I wanted to see them naked, to see them as like other men. Not so as to stop taking them seriously as intellects (I never did), but so as to feel my own power in relation to them.*

Especially for a woman pursuing the life of the mind, writes Gallop, *desire is a blessing rather than an insult. My desire gave me drive and energy; being an object of desire made me feel admired and wanted, worthy and lovable.*

Or maybe it's something else. *Do you think Farnsworth was a starfucker?* laughs a professor and friend. I tell him it's what made the architect so angry in the end. *I was already famous, and she is now famous throughout the world!* bellowed the architect in the famous trial in which they sue each other.

4.

I am led to a glass room in the Newberry Library, to a series of cardboard boxes that contain her: notebooks full of tangled handwriting that span decades, dozens of folders full of typewritten poems and letters, and photographs. The archivists stay on their own side of the glass. They are the only other women here, and they watch me as I unfold our history.

There is no beginning to her unpublished memoirs. There are chapter headings, and there is a flow of handwriting across several journals. I pick up her blue journal first: on each right-hand page, one continuous block of handwriting from top to bottom. On each left-hand page, orphaned fragments of sentences, clarifications and second thoughts, or just a word. Her handwriting is cursive but straight up and down, and every letter takes up almost the same amount of space. She is strangely judicious as she writes. The paper is as thin as onion skin between my gloved fingers.

If there is a proper way to write this history of a glass house, I don't want to know. I want to hold each phrase as she held it, to know its weight, a spontaneous thought on the surface of the mind arriving out of the body's memory.

I work slowly, consuming each sentence, typing it in my laptop as I read it silently
it is clear to see that I acted, that my shadow fell somewhere
and it comes out my fingers. I vacate myself and I simply transcribe, sentence by sentence. I do not find heartbreak; or at least, what I find I do not recognize as the heartbreak inflicted by a love interest. These are not even memories. They are visions.

There is a strange chronology to her unpublished memoirs that feels mostly associative. Or, as her estranged sister would put it, *Edith's memoirs* had such gaps that I was not able to put them in order with any continuity. I imagine the illness with prolonged periods of weakness had something to do with it. These spaces between are treated as suspicious; the nonlinear, non-chronological is seen as chaos, perhaps evidence of a feeble mind.

Edith begins her memoirs with a fire that burns thirty years before she is born: *wonderful to think of,* she writes, imagining her grandparents and mother fleeing Chicago as it burns at their heels—the first of many fires of her childhood. Where is her father? Nowhere in the room as she hovers over a picture book of famous ships laid open on the floor, a vessel sinking in flames, its drowning crew slipping from the fire into the *dark, eternal depths.*

She calls its impression on her a *stab.*

And she feels it, she feels herself hurtling through that opening in the world.

Then, on the next page, she is in a car speeding through a tunnel along the autostrada in Rome, thrown through its dilating aperture into the blazing pure yellow of sun.

She flinches as the moment explodes and disintegrates.

I found myself deeply and unaccountably shaken.

————

It shouldn't be this way, but I'm afraid that this story is going to end badly, a friend warns her during the process of designing this house. I mark up a Xerox form and paperclip it to this passage in her journal to remind myself of this fact.

This is a research document.

It is also an accounting of relationships.

————

I want to ask her about what I find in her journal, her translations of a poet who spent his childhood blind. I want to ask her why she chose these lines:

> Soften these stones
> Open my eyes
> Blind
>   made of coal
> And   full of thistles

Or I would like to tell her that for a time, she was my only correspondent. In this neighborhood where her archive lives, at the bottom of a canyon of glass towers, cell phone service is spotty. I talk rarely, if at all, with anybody. I have noticed that when I do, my voice is softer, that I want so much to connect with the person on the other end that everything they say has brighter edges to it.

I have always wanted to ask her, *Did the poet ever tell you when his blindness lifted? Did you ask him to describe the first light that he saw? Did it outweigh his fear? Or are we better left in the dark?*

These are the questions I ask lying in a twin bed in a bedroom that I have rented for $500 from friends of a friend while I do this archival work, trying to sleep under a hole in the ceiling that water has rotted away. The hole is black and gives no sense of how deep it is, its edges brown, soft, and crumbling. A sheet of plastic is secured over all of it to catch small pieces of plaster as they fall. I keep the window open at night since there is no air-conditioning. The plastic sheet rises and falls, as if the hole is breathing.

When she is not putting her life into chronological-associative order, she writes strange poetry in which an abyss appears. But stranger still are the poems I find within her poems, scratching away at my Xerox copies in the semi-dark, listening to the hole in the ceiling breathe.

I looked about me
It seemed to me that a long hand
would stretch out from the ceiling
and draw me up into the dark
like a feather snatched by the wind.

By morning
I had forgotten everything

———

I am an unfunded scholar here, a piece of misplaced furniture among the recognized, invited researchers with real projects, projects with titles and deadlines. The grant I had applied for was rejected with a line that the reviewer may not have realized I would read: *She just wants to use this time to write, that's not what this grant is for.* This grant is for the people slumped over the tables around me: scholars who have come to see the library's collection of seventeenth- and eighteenth-century European maps.

But the Newberry Library is public. And anyone who arrives in time to claim a table is provided one, regardless of grant status. Each morning, I walk up the marble stairs, research attendants already flying by on the second floor, the third, making my way up to the fourth. Every person who passes me smells a different temperature than I am, cool, slightly perfumed, like they've slept in the same archival tissue and glassine that their research documents are kept in. A woman on the stairs leans away slightly as I pass her, the heat of two buses I took to arrive here from the South Side still rolling off me. I feel the chilled edges of her against me, though I am four feet away.

Each morning, I have been working for an hour by the time the grant-funded scholar from Italy arrives, too late to claim a table, pounding her fists and yelling, pointing into the room in which I work. She knows. She knows that I am just a member of the unwashed public taking up precious, air-conditioned space.

I bend over my laptop and hold my breath until she exits my peripheral vision.

———

One morning when I am alone in the apartment on Chicago's South Side, enjoying a rare moment of solitude while my roommates are at work, I Google the phone number of Edith's only living relative, a nephew. It's listed. I call and am almost astonished when he answers the phone. He doesn't understand why anyone would want to know about his aunt. I ask him whether she and the architect had a romantic relationship to his knowledge. *Oh, I don't think so*, he tells me. *He was so quiet. She brought him to a family dinner once, and he just sat there like a lump.*

Historians will tell us that his silence is the silence of heroes. The glass house is valued for its silence. Here, we have only the words of men who write about buildings. The house was, as described by historian Fritz Neumeyer in *The Artless Word*, no longer merely a place for living but a site dedicated to *contemplating nature and holding a silent dialogue with the world*. The same book says that in 1950, with the design of this house, the architect began *a process of emptying space* that ushered forth a series of glass buildings with large, open, interior volumes, first in the United States, then abroad. In America, the architect himself would describe his efforts as *battles of spirit*.

In other words, this glass house was among his first in a series of silent, empty rooms.

I have no idea what kind of silence the architect imagined, because he himself would never offer a word on the subject. *He felt that the house had never really been understood*, says another historian, Kevin Harrington, but what is meant to be understood remains unsaid.

Perhaps we can simply note the fact that as a young man, the architect preferred to sleep on a mattress in his bathtub, leaving the main room of his studio apartment an empty space in which to meditate on empty space.

This silence is often taken as material evidence of the architect's love of the writings of Catholic philosopher Romano Guardini, who wrote that man's fear of empty space and silence is the fear of being alone with God *and the forlorn standing in front of him*, a confrontation that man attempts to avoid.

That is why he always wants to have things, pictures, words, and sounds around himself.

There are some theories that the Christian theology of silence has simple origins: Saint Ambrose reading silently to himself so as to listen to the inner teacher. Augustine describes this in his *Confessions*, long considered the first autobiography. It is shocking because he addresses God directly, writing into his hermetical silence, calling God *you*.

———

If I could speak directly to her, this is what I would say:

It is strange that I pursue you, because most of the time, all I want is to be alone.

And when I am alone all day with your papers, I begin to believe that you are speaking to me—or I find my own thoughts in your strangely glimmering observations.

An expert in hermeticism explains on the radio that if we are left alone too long, the first thing that happens is that sensations become hypersensorial: *porridge really tastes like porridge*.

And then we hallucinate: a voice arrives.

I have continued to wait for yours.

———

Did she want to be alone? There is a part of me that believes that she did. Why else would she build this house on the Fox River, far away from the more affluent Chicago suburbs? I tend toward the theory of being alone, but I am descended from many women who chose this. Sometimes the choice found them: on my mother's side, the great-aunt whose husband was shot in a fight over a card game; she spent the rest of her life collecting dogs, pets, and rifles at their house in rural eastern Nebraska, hosting weekend fishing trips for family at a nearby lake. In the summers, as children, we would sleep in the cabin where Dubay was murdered. Nobody remembered his first name, and the furniture never changed since the day he was shot there: the same card table, the same heavy, mildewed, and moth-eaten bed. Its springs and frame reeking of rust, the scurrying sounds of mice multiplying in the dark corners.

A woman's choice to live alone: part circumstance, perhaps part instinct.

I think Edith describes this particular kind of being alone best. She feels it for the first time during a decade that she spends vacillating between Europe, where she is studying violin and traveling, and the United States, which she leaves at nineteen when she drops out of her undergraduate education at the University of Chicago. She refers to these years as a period of *vague expansion*, and she commits herself to it. Standing on the deck of a ship, she finds that she is

released
from dimensions that I was used to thinking of as mine.
So wide, so long, so thick and with certain traits thrown in,
but always through the refractions of other people's eyes.

But now
*   there was nothing to limit one's transcending.*

Historians will reduce her early years of vague expansion to this: *During her violin studies in Rome, she learned that she could not face an audience.* They will not acknowledge that the audience offered to her are men: the violin teacher and Italian concert virtuoso Mario Corti, who takes an apartment above hers, who listens to her practice, who yells out his window when she stops to take a walk, the one who catches her at the entrance of the building to say, *I have been waiting. I want to say something to you. I love you with all of my heart. Do you know what that means, to love with all of one's heart?*

I do not know whether she answers.

She travels out of Italy for a few weeks and encounters a man who insists that she meet him in the courtyard of the Alhambra one evening so that he can lead her to one of the balconies where she will play violin for him. *I will be waiting*, he says.

Whether afraid of failure or of success . . . I went to bed, she writes.

————

At times, being alone seems to be the inevitable condition. In my early twenties, during a semester studying abroad in Rome, I make an afternoon stop in the art supply store and the owner reaches out for my hand. *The two buildings. I am so sorry.* I walk to our studio building, greeted by our professor's voice echoing down the stairs, *sono canadese! Sono canadese!* He is passing out little red maple leaves to sew onto our backpacks, practicing with us a call and response—*sono canadese, I am Canadian*—that he believes will make us safe, immune from harm. He tells us we cannot return to the United States. *The American experiment is over; call your parents.*

The next day, shops sell magazines with photographs of people peering from and leaping through the broken facades of the World Trade Center towers, their descent mirrored in the glass. They fall once as a body, once as a reflection, and countless times in the magazines. They never stop falling. They are still falling.

The other study abroad programs return to the United States. We stay. We have one telephone at school and take turns trying to call our parents to let them know. I keep dialing the digits from the phone card over and over, listening to the prompts, pressing 9, pressing 1, pressing ten digits, waiting, a busy tone. AT&T was my mother's first national client for her voice business, and it is her calm voice telling me to press the same digits over and over again to connect, the same voice I cannot reach, the first voice I ever heard, now robotic, making me scream into the phone, *MOM, PLEASE*, every time the call disconnects.

————

When she leaves Europe as a young woman, Edith writes that it is because *the pleasure of drawing close to what had been remote, of becoming fond of what was distant, left me abruptly and completely.*

She returns to the United States in the early 1930s, as Hitler is rising to power in Germany. She has already witnessed Mussolini's ascent. (Meanwhile, I am writing this in a version of the United States in which no matter who is in power, refugee children are incarcerated in cages at the US-Mexico border. I teach at a university that has done little to prepare me for the possibility of ICE raids on campus and have learned from my students that the best way to prevent the seizure of one of them out of my classroom is a group hug—all of us throwing our bodies on the person ICE has come to take.)

The America she is returning to is also one that has a hard time facing facts. She meets a Swiss physician on board the SS *Berlin* as she sails across the Atlantic, a man who is bothered by the fact that, he claims, American doctors don't tell their patients that they have cancer; instead, they allow the same patient to go from hospital to hospital, specialist to specialist, seeking treatment with no idea.

She tells him it is because Americans insist on happy endings, and that for an American, *the happiest of endings is no ending at all.*

When she returns to the United States, she records the experience of having her poetry books put away in the closet and her tennis racket handed to her like this:

I have become a graft on my own root.

———

When they collect us in the dark, when they load us into a van that will take us to the airport to fly back to the United States, we are all crying. None of us wants to go. We had believed that the experiment was over.

When we return to school, the university has given us what they consider to be the best studio spaces for architecture students. They are at the top of a five-floor concrete building with an uninterrupted row of operable windows running along one wall. Every day, I sit down at my desk next to the gravity and the blue, the promise of falling. Most of the students choose desks in the middle of the room.

What happened to you? asks my professor. *Did you fall in love over there? You're so spaced out.*

How to say that I cannot draw a building without thinking of what it symbolizes, without imagining a plane running into it, bodies leaping out of it, cannot sit at my desk without feeling the tug of gravity beyond the window?

Yes, I say. *Love.*

If love is a discourse of absence, which it often is, then I was in fact giving shape to absence, elaborating its fiction, by staring out the window.

5.

Researching a woman who would build a glass house for herself is a particular kind of being alone. It is the alone of sitting in a unit in one of the architect's elegant Lake Shore Drive apartment buildings in Chicago, one of twin glass towers he designed (after the glass house, he devoted himself to glass towers). It is the alone of wading through four thousand pages of the trial transcript *van der Rohe vs. Farnsworth* in which the architect sued her for fees he had no contract enforcing and that were piled on after she had already paid today's equivalent of nearly one million dollars for the one-room house. (She countersued him for fraud, since the house leaked water from the roof, flooding the whole interior.) It is the alone of staring at all of these pages, having been informed by the man who inexplicably possesses the only copy of them that I can sit and read as long as I'd like but am not allowed to photograph them or take them with me. It is the alone of simultaneously acknowledging the impossibility of this task and giving up on it, choosing instead to stare across this table and into the adjacent and identical all-glass tower where—in an apartment exactly like this one—a completely naked man watches television.

———

By 1947, she believes that the house he is designing for her will be a prototype for new American architecture, that postwar America will contain many glass houses, whole subdivisions of glass houses, and indeed this seems to have been a possibility still when Robert Hall McCormick III hires the same architect to build his house, completed in 1952. He envisions this house becoming a model for the rest of the houses in the Chicago suburb of Elmhurst. But after one such attempt at this, he quits. The house has no basement, no air-conditioning, and it looks strange.

———

And maybe the fact that what he is designing for her is a glass house—a house that will require endless labor to clean and maintain, that will offer little privacy or security—simply slips past her, busy in the hospital, being assigned not only the patients that need to be cured of the fatal kidney disease nephritis but also any patient having a mental breakdown.

It is two in the morning, a Sunday, when her telephone rings. The voice on the other end is *quiet* and *infinitely sad*. She agrees to meet him at the hospital.

She sits next to him and carries on conversation until morning, interrupted only by the moments when the man pounds his head against the rails of the bed. He is her first private patient.

Next time, the eminent neurologist says to her in the break room, *demand to see the tongue. Say, "Show me your tongue!" Most people are used to doctors who examine tongues. Say, "I am the doctor; you are the patient. I shall cure you."*

She hesitates.

No, do not learn what agonizes them.

The recounting of pain only serves to convert it into a work of art, a monument.

———

The house was a work of art, a monument, from the moment its first lines were put to paper. It seemed to have sprung whole from the architect's mind as a glass bubble fighting gravity, columns tethering it in place, framing a canopy of trees. In the infamous watercolor drawing, the ground is one straight graphite line. Or perhaps I have misunderstood the drawing, and the line is in fact the surface of the river, blank and rising.

If so, it is a prescient drawing, since the river would rise during construction in 1950, flooding just to the floor of the house—here it is, a boat anchored in place, the river rushing past it, a mirror of the gray and empty sky. This flood happens on a cold, windy day—the branches of the bare trees shaking so fast that in this photograph of it, they are nothing but a dark blur, the forest just a tangle of black on the other side of the glass house, which is empty, transparent. Everything in this photograph vibrates except the house; it is entirely still, its white lines against all nature.

The essayist Richard Sennett once found himself at a party in the very glass tower in which I first encountered the trial transcript. Sennett writes that he was unable to tear himself away from the floor-to-ceiling windows, that he found them *fatally attractive: the tall buildings thrust up into nothingness, their very height creating an abyss below. . . . A person who suddenly feels he has had enough might press his face yearningly against the glass, yet he is protected by a material which lets him see everything inaccessible to desire.*

———

There would be other ways to learn the abyss, to enter into it. I try wading out into Lake Michigan. On this little strip of lakefront beach on the South Side, there are high school seniors in boats wearing life vests and sunglasses prepared to direct swimmers back to the shore. Their boats delineate the

FIGURE 4. Flooding at the Farnsworth House, 1950.

boundary of safety but build up a rapport with them, and the boundary moves a little farther out. From this edge, with my stainless-steel mug full of white wine, I tip back and float with my ears beneath the surface of the lake. I only hear what the lake has to tell me, which is the ancient story of water.

When I try to stand up, I find that the sand is no longer beneath me. I tread water and sip from the mug.

I do this at the end of each day, and I stare out to where the water meets the sky in one thin line. When the wine is gone, I slip my head back so that the water and silence flow in.

The upper-class white bubbles of space the architect created were not limited to rarified apartments in the city—far from where I float—and houses in the suburbs beyond Chicago; his campus plan for IIT, where he was chair of the department of architecture, began destroying Bronzeville in the late 1940s—a thriving Black community that rivaled Harlem as a cultural center. At a moment when social policy and law demanded racial integration in the United States, architects and those who could afford to hire them found a way around it—displacement, denial, destruction. The thin innocence of a sheet of glass wrapping around each of his buildings would reveal none of the violence these buildings enacted on the world around them.

———

Edith could afford to leave this city on weekends. When she did, she was joined by cars advancing in long lines on the interstate, driving west, heading toward the horizon. She tried to imagine those driving them—*their hands clutching their steering wheels*—and for what reasons, she asks? *For wives, children, lawns to be mowed, weeds to be pulled?* She describes them as her companions, *for whom this book has been written and to whom it is dedicated without reproach.* This is the closest I have come to finding an acknowledgment that she saw the memoirs as a work, as a book—one she began late in life, perhaps realizing that she would have to describe her life for others, that she might someday be a subject. Perhaps feeling, among these families, like an anomaly.

Rather than rites—marriages, children—she seems to want to go through transformations. She was not alone in this. I am holding a typewritten draft of the first few chapters of Katharine Butler Hathaway's *The Little Locksmith*. It lives in Edith's archive. I turn the cover page over in this glass-walled room. It opens:

I have an island in the palm of my right hand. It is quite large and shaped like an almond.

And a few pages later:

Thus begins the story of my house.

In Edith's memoirs, Katharine Butler Hathaway describes this to her as the *story of my transformations.*

House is transformation. Born to a wealthy family in 1890, Hathaway spent her childhood strapped to a weighted harness and forced to lie flat in an effort to straighten the effects of spinal tuberculosis. She was unbound at fifteen years old, only to discover that her body was the size of a ten-year-old child's and her spine was still extremely curved. Despite this, she attended Radcliffe College and purchased her own home in Castine, Maine, in 1921, not far from Gray Gables, where Edith's family spent summers. Hathaway's house would allow her to write and draw, to visit with family, to play with her nieces and nephews, to take a lover—a place that would not impose its time on her but a place in which her writing and her life would exist side by side.

I try to imagine it, one eye on the clock, fussing with these words in the afternoon, aware of the archive closing at 5:00 p.m., the two buses I will need to take to get back to the apartment, the long and exhausted wait toward sunset, being quiet in my rented space in the middle of someone else's life.

Edith's memory of Hathaway as simply her friend, Katharine, is hard to place in time. Katharine was committed to a life of *singular delicacy and seclusion*, as Edith describes it, something she admires. In her memoirs, they sit in the front seat of a car, dishes of peach ice cream and pages of this manuscript spread between them. Katharine holds up her hand. The fate line splits in the center of it and converges again, as if *fate were exploded in the middle life into something entirely new and strange and then folded together again to go on as quietly as it began.*

You see, Katharine writes, *the story of my house is the story of my liberation as a human being.*
So let me tell you what had made me prisoner.

Later, Edith writes that she does not believe that what Katharine is experiencing is truly a transformation. If it is, she believes it is *due to the inventiveness of the author*, she writes in her journal. This is not a story of transformation, she argues with herself, but a story of her *unrequited love for life.*

———

Katharine is nowhere to be found in the photograph I have on my desk showing young women clustered on a rock in Castine, the only photographic evidence I can find of Edith's social set in this place. Edith's appearance suggests that she's relaxed among these women. The year is 1926, making her likely about twenty-two years old: she has just returned

FIGURE 5. Women at a picnic in coastal Maine: M.G.P. (Mary "Polly" Porter), Alicia Rosenbaum, Dorothy Blake, Edith Farnsworth, Dodo Blake, and Katherine Lindsay, Summer 1926.

to the United States after two years studying violin in Italy. She would leave for Europe again within a year. The photograph lists the women's names at the bottom: *M.G.P., Alicia, D. Blake, E. Farnsworth, Dodo, K.L.* The six women are picnicking, their flat shoes coated in mud—a strange contrast to their stockings and skirts—smoking cigarettes in cardigans and coats.

Was there another life tucked inside the life that Edith narrates in her memoirs? She spent time with Katharine in Paris in the late 1920s, where they lived in apartments near each other on the Left Bank, and then went their separate ways: Edith would have been in her late twenties, Katharine Butler—not yet Hathaway—in her late thirties. They do not reunite for years, a passage of time marked by a simple phrase in Edith's memoirs: *And then finally*, as in, *And then finally I heard that Katharine had married somebody by the name of Daniel Hathaway and gone to live in Blue Hill.* There are no other mentions of Katharine after this.

I took a ^ different—Edith crosses out the word "tenderer"—*less fanciful* view of this *story of transformations.*

6.

I cannot afford a house that will transform me, but I take solace in the walls that I rent, the verticality and the numbness. I sketch interventions into walls, ones that would allow a finger to slip inside or a whole hand. I imagine a wall that could envelope me, a wall that would contain the secret of itself when others were in the room. A wall that answers the question that the architect asked once in a lecture, almost a century before I am born: *who still feels anything of a wall, an opening?*

———

A glass house cannot retain heat. She stands in her office and puts a hand up to the window. Leaves are just starting to turn gold, the evenings darker. Her hand grows cold almost immediately and she pulls it away, sliding it back into her jacket pocket. Heat exits the body and travels toward any cooler surface, the human thermodynamics of empathy, as if the body forgets to keep itself warm first, as if skin is an open door.

Think of it as *letting the outside in*, he suggests to her.

Everything outside makes its way into the body. It takes just a simple hormone, cortisol, to survive almost any shock. Without it, expose a rat to cold and he will die from stress. Administer just a little bit of it, though, and he will shiver but not die. This is survival.

When a body cannot produce cortisol, it can be extracted from other bodies. For this, she discovers that there is a meat packing plant in Chicago where the pituitary glands are extracted from hogs, collected in a metal bucket, and frozen. These are used to make a synthetic version of the adrenocorticotropic hormone which controls the production of cortisol. Edith calls and asks for a sample.

———

She enters a conference room to present this research, one packed to the doors and rigged with bristling loudspeakers and amplifiers. She can barely see the scores and scores of faces in the dark, the pipes gripped in their teeth. She hears *focus a little more sharply, please* when the screen transmits radiant digits that blur, and *speak a little louder, please* when the amplifier around her neck begins to bray, emitting a voice of its own.

She describes the children she's treated, the ones chronically ill with nephritis—their kidneys malfunctioning, their bodies swelling, the younger siblings who play under their gurneys, unaware.

She explains how to cure the body by flooding it with its own miracle drug.

———

I find my seat in the dark conference room. When it is my turn to present, I trace the history of the vacant piece of land in Saint Louis on which I'd tried to perform my own fall. Beneath me, embedded in the earth, the debris of the imploded structures. I talk about everything the news footage didn't capture, the residents who had been moved into structures on the periphery of this public housing project while they were forced to watch the towers they used to live in destroyed, falling to the ground in sheets of dust and brick. Just as I say the words *then there was nothing*, the power blinks out: total darkness, projection vanished.

I stand there while the two moderators scramble at my feet, groping for cords, and everyone flicks on their phones, faces illuminated.

The rest of the afternoon, I pinball between rooms intermittently flooded with projected graphs and images in the basement of the conference hotel, drinking the free coffee until my heart races and I black out a little every time I stand up to change one dark, crowded room for another.

When I need to feel the warmth of the sun, I step outside the hotel and pretend to check my email on my phone, which is also teetering toward darkness, its screen blinking on and off because I've dropped it too many times. I see the professor who taught the studio years ago in which I'd pushed my desk against the window, the studio that had me dreaming about falling, about gravity. He takes my hand in his and squeezes it, pumps it up and down while he exclaims, *A real job! You have a real job!* I nod dully.

After this encounter, I avoid the gravity of all men at this conference, preferring to drift in and out of darkness. Under my jacket and under my handshake is a black dress cut away to reveal the part of me that I know is the most beautiful, my back. Sitting in the dark, I feel the scratch of the cheap upholstered conference chairs on my skin through the thin fabric of my jacket, which doesn't insulate me from anything here.

———

Maybe it's true, what she wrote: *the refined joys of the mind in solitude promptly deteriorate under the risks and indignities of publicity.*

When her presentation is over, she stands in the hallway, her ears still ringing while people mill around her, asking questions about her research. A man presses in. *Finish answering the questions, and join me for lunch.*

The logic of the conference is the logic of getting tenure, which is tied to the logic of keeping our professional association afloat, which means bending research to the logic of capital, and so the presentations had made very little sense. A giant ball of plastic bottles rolling around in the desert to build awareness of the plastic islands in the ocean, something about fungus, and a bridge built of ant bodies that all share one brain—*what if we built like these ants?* the man with the prestigious research position had asked, and I imagined reaching out, holding the legs of the woman in front of me, and she the woman in front of her, a human chain, a shared brain.

The woman next to me at the bar tosses her hair, and I feel it brush my back. It is a relief to be reminded that I belong to the world of the physical, a world in which drinking corresponds with a certain type of lucidity.

When Edith returned from her conference, the men who had questioned her were already demanding volumes of pituitary glands from her suppliers, jeopardizing her research. *Haven't you any instinct for self-preservation? Don't tell all of your secrets to everyone who asks you,* yelled the man in charge of this supply.

Even the architect was not immune to such opportunists: Philip Johnson would visit Mies in his office while he designed her glass house and tell him that it was impossible. Johnson would then copy his idea, completing the structure quickly so that his was the first glass house in America. He built it for himself.

Possible. Not possible. Possible. Not possible. A man and a woman sit at opposite ends of the dining table in her glass house. This is a film of a performance piece, but it has the awkward appeal of watching a bad date. The man jerks his head left, says *possible*, and right, says *not possible*. He turns his head back and forth this way, constantly, intermittently slamming his palm into the table. The woman faces him, watching and saying nothing. Eventually, she gets up to leave the house, and he remains at the table, talking to himself. The performance piece continues, but I close the window on my computer because I am also bored with him.

FIGURE 6. *Modern Living.*

7.

A man I slept with years ago emails me to tell me that he's building a building. He gives me its coordinates on land, as if I would understand what these precise numbers mean. After some research, I find that there is not just one, but there are many systems for abstracting our curved earth into a flat, projected surface, one that can be quantified, sold. Choosing which system to use is a matter of deciding how much distortion of reality is acceptable.

I'm tempted to respond with coordinates of my own, but I am not in a fixed position these days. I am everywhere. The drain in my apartment becomes slower. I twist my hair to put it up, and I notice a bald spot the size of a baseball behind my left ear.

I comb my hair down over both ears.

———

Occasionally, the people we have been intimate with reach out to us. What do we do with this sudden violation of space and time?

I sit in my office during office hours, listening to my students recount their problems, which are primarily caused by the predatory natures of both the city and the university: they are broke, they can't pay their rent, they can't pay their credit card bills or their fees, they are pregnant, they are not pregnant, their friend has been diagnosed with "the blood cancer." *Leukemia?* I ask.

No, the H.I.B., the young man whispers softly, as language breaks around his sorrow. I am too old not to be bilingual, too much his professor to ask him how close he is with his friend, if he needs to be tested. Instead, I say, *It's so important that your friend goes to the doctor. Does he have a doctor?* He shakes his head and his eyes water. I realize that this conference is not for advice but for space, for witness. I teach another class in twenty minutes. We sit quietly in my office, each of us looking at our own folded hands. The surfaces of the department-mandated furniture are all white, a clinical appearance that in this moment is completely useless, cruel. He says *thank you*, reaches over to squeeze my hand and leaves. His words remain in my office, suspended in the dying afternoon light.

———

Of spring burning in falling sentences, she writes in a poem she omits from her never-published collection.

———

Would I write to her about this? Would I write to her about the cost per square foot of the apartment I can hardly afford to rent, which has increased exponentially in value despite the scuffs I have made on the wall, the sawdust that has collected on the floor from when the man who came to install the internet drilled into it, the unconscious man found bleeding from the nose in an overstuffed chair in the lobby? Would I write to her about the prospective tenants I have watched being brought into the building past the bloodstained chair, which has simply been turned to face the wall, or the small dog that runs in circles down the first-floor hallway and urinates on the carpet near the mailboxes? And whose dog is it?

How would she feel about that, our lives bumping together, both of us translated into the world of character, plot, action, if I were to write to her directly?

Before she abandoned a career as a violinist, she abandoned a career as a novelist; she felt that her financial comfort left her little to say about the average human experience.

It seems to me, at times, that I have attached myself to her because I believe proximity means she might rub off on me, that I might be similarly unaffected, released into a world in which the beginning of summer does not mean the start of lean months, no work but reading, sweating, cheese and apples for dinner. What is it that draws us to others' wealth, that believes still in the delusion of upward mobility by proximity to them, even when they're gone? Their life cannot also be ours. In fact, it is only our poverty that makes their comfort possible. Perhaps the desire I feel is not for her but for the hours we have lost in materializing her wealth.

When I am confronted with the smell of shag carpet and the glow of watery light through a white curtain in the house provided during a monthlong artist residency, it becomes a series of unassailable facts: a couch upholstered in goldenrod yellow velvet, a lumpy brown easy chair, dark wood cabinets with faux medieval hardware, the thin vein of gold that runs through every cream-colored surface, my pale face in the mirror.

It looks as if someone is about to return home. Someone who is not me and in fact very different from me, someone perhaps more attached to the idea of the undisturbed sitting room, and for this reason I cannot begin to imagine cutting into the walls in the way that I had proposed in my residency application.

Instead, I sit next to the largest window in the house, and I write. Everything I write comes out water. I flood the glass house over and over, the river rising and snapping the great sheets of glass, the river sweeping through the house in the way that water does, effortless and brutal at once.

She chooses the river before she chooses the house, and I cannot forget this, do not want to diminish the fact that her earliest visits were to this living thing. Nor do I know what to do with the fact that her father died of a heart attack while crossing a body of water on a hunting trip, folding in on himself in a small boat that carried him to the other side just before she purchased this land.

What to do with the fact that nobody purchases a river? That a river is a boundary we respect, that we cannot monetize except in proximity to it. But the river can decide to be done with us. The river can decide to destroy us in an instant.

I wake to the sound of sheets of rain running off the roof.

I think that was the beginning, says one of the old men who worked with the architect as a young man, speaking as if the river gave birth to the house. I am trying to remember if he is the one I've always heard was drunk most of the time, an unreliable narrator.

———

The last day that I spend writing water ends with a walk down the shoulder of the littered highway. The nearest bar is in a neighboring town, Lincoln City. On my right are speeding cars, and on my left a cliff crumbling into Siletz Bay. The only other person at the bar is an older man in riding leathers who asks me how I am doing. I begin to tell him I am writing a book, fighting back tears that surprise me, that start streaming down my face, the river inside of me leaking out. *No, no*, he says, unable to look at me but also unable to leave because he has a full beer in front of him. While the bartender backs away, I put my head on the bar, mortified. Without looking directly at me, the gray man in riding leathers reaches over and thumps me on my back as if I were a broken television. *I bet it's some good shit*, he says. *Some really good shit.*

After this, I don't try to write anymore. Instead, I go into the garage next to the house. It is unattached to time, a dark space. The floor of the garage is covered in insect carcasses and leaves, illuminated by the warm sun of late summer coming in from under the door. I'm vaguely aware of the old bikes and the tools and loose bricks that are crammed into the darker corners. I will improvise. I will collapse time. Here on this thin piece of scrim that I hang from one of the ceiling beams, I'll project images of her glass house at full scale. I will climb into them. I will stop seeking to write about the house and will begin living in the pale tracings of it.

The sterile glow of a university-issued projector dims the house's white-painted steel structure to gray. Each image shows the mostly empty one-room house with just a few pieces of furniture at odd angles: chairs that face each other on either side of the front door or crammed together in a sitting room near a small coffee table holding an oversized vase filled with erratic wildflowers. Each image emphasizes its transparency, framing the trees or the sky on the other side of the house; as if the whole point of the glass house were not staying but going, getting elsewhere.

The problem with these first-published images of the house is the problem with almost all architectural photographs, which is that they are vacant—as

FIGURE 7. *Glass House (Projection).*

though the photographer intends the viewer to understand the building as existing in some pre- or post-human world, as though the building was designed for some place from which we are banished or to which we have not yet arrived.

There is no woman in these photographs of the house, so I become her. I stand behind the scrim panel and allow the light from the projector to wash over my body. I try to align myself with the image, which is difficult as I am staring into the light of the projector, trying to discern the pixelated edge of the house from that of a tree. I hover just behind the scrim, belonging neither to the garage nor to the house, nor to the present, nor to the past.

In one photograph I particularly love, her mattress lies on the white marble floor of the glass house. It is covered with what appears to be a wool blanket, and its pillowcase is smoothed with precision. It is as matter-of-fact as it is incongruous, like camping in a temple.

I throw a pillow on the filthy ground of the garage. I take off all my clothes, and I curl up naked on the floor, my back to the camera. I am trying to understand if empathy is possible. I do not know how we can write history otherwise.

8.

How the house was intended to be built was invented as it was being built. What it was celebrated for, in the end, was the way that every bit of structure was concealed, elusive, not what it appeared to be—an innovative process of effacement that made the house appear to effortlessly float, a process that took weeks to calculate and months to build. The architect's genius is concealed in this house, beneath the many decisions that were made by the people he hired to complete the work.

Progress was slow. And construction was slow. She felt *caught between two horizontal planes*, she wrote. For another two years, she waited. Things finally began to emerge from the ground, but they were confusing.

When historians write about the construction of this house, they describe it as if it were magic—*what we see, we cannot believe*. It is something to celebrate, this *structural trickery*, in the words of Michael Cadwell. How the building meets the earth is unclear—the exterior columns are buried in concrete footings underground, so all we see are slender steel pins disappearing into the earth. The same columns support the floor and roof, but how they do so is impossible to see: they seem to slip right by these heavy planes, just kissing the edges of them. In his analysis, Cadwell discovers evidence that what connects them—plug welds that fuse the vertical columns to the floor and roof—are sanded over, painted with a flat white enamel, obliterated. The author scolds anyone frustrated by this trick—*what the steel frame is need not concern us. This is a search for essences.*

How does one experience these essences? She visits the house during construction and is accompanied by a young man who has invited himself along, a man who wants to meet the architect. He begins shouting:

Do you think we've slipped out of orbit? After so many years in the same one?

She turns to follow his gaze, to see what he sees. Something floats in the sky above them, but it is pink and looming too close. Is it the sun? She feels she could almost reach out and touch it. It emits no heat, only light. Standing on the white marble platform of her unfinished house, anything seems possible. The exposed marble beneath her feet glows.

But really, do you think we've slipped out of orbit? After so many years in the same one?

I go to the Museum of Modern Art where a man named Paul feeds me photographs from the Mies van der Rohe archive—the official, historical, and institutional collection of the architect. I may only photograph the photographs, and I may only do it at this table, which is under a blaring fluorescent light so bright that it is a blinding streak shooting across every glossy black-and-white photograph. In each photograph I take, the glass house appears to be exploding, melting into a ball of fire.

What are these for? asks Paul, peering over my shoulder as I upload them onto my laptop.

It's research, I snap at him.

There are no photographs of her here. In one image, a different woman sits inside the glass house. She turns to look over her shoulder to meet the photographer's gaze, but she does not smile. I photograph her and the smear of fire almost obliterates her face.

I took a red-eye flight to get here. I have no research time to speak of, teaching four days a week, so I had called in sick to the other side of the

FIGURE 8. *Glass House (Beth)*.

country when I landed this morning. I am so tired that my skin hurts. On my way out of the museum, I drop my phone on the black marble floor. The screen is cobwebbed with cracks. It flickers on, a hypnotic blue, a constant color. Nothing else.

––––––

Do you think we've slipped out of orbit? After so many years in the same one?
The young architect asks again, now panicking, turning to the architect of the glass house. The man had just arrived from England to see this house under construction, traveling thousands of miles to this field where the order of the universe has begun to collapse.
How the hell should I know? the architect yells back.

Once the phenomenon is traced back to wildfires in Canada, she returns to her complaints about the house emerging from the ground. *There is already a local rumor that it is a tuberculosis sanitarium.*

––––––

Phone obliterated. All I have to stare at now is my notebook.

––––––

The architect had invited her to his house for dinner once. She arrived to an empty space: a drawing table in the dining room, a living room with a couch but nowhere to eat. She heard sounds in the kitchen, and she followed the dark hallway toward them.

––––––

Imagine if some of the things I have read are true: that the doctor allowed the architect to keep a key to the house, that in a sense, though they didn't occupy it at the same time, it was both of theirs. There was a play performed at the glass house that contained a scene to this effect: the doctor arrives at her glass house only to find Lora Marx, the architect's longtime companion, wandering around in nothing but the architect's white oxford shirt.
The audience was appalled. They could not believe the architect was being imagined in this way. They believed that the architect was above sex, or above sex in glass houses, or above lending his shirt to his lover.
The scenario is, in my mind, plausible and not altogether unappealing.

But the same audiences would not mind the women he had sex with being reimagined. Of either of the two famous American women he slept with during the process of building the glass house, this is what the architect's first biographer concluded:

1. Lora Marx *proved to be the kind of woman he could tolerate having around for a long time. And she put up with his occasional peccadillos.*
   Also, *she played no role in his creativity, as either inspiration or irritant.*
2. Mary Callery was a woman *with whom in the course of the next decade he carried on the kind of light, desultory romantic affair to which he was accustomed in the old country.* This sentence occurs no more than three inches under the heading "America: The Triumph of Steel and Glass, 1949–58," in the architect's biography.

And yet, it was he they tolerated, not the other way around. Marx found Mies's presence to be interruptive to her creative life. And Mies once said to Mary Callery, for whom he was designing an art studio, *you stay in the kitchen, that's where women should be.* The man reporting this laughs: *we thought she was going to beat him, I'll tell you that.*

———

I in my sleeping space and he in his, Edith wrote, explaining how she imagined she would invite a guest to sleep in her glass house without rooms. *Unless,* she adds, *sheer depression and discomfort should drive us together.*

Who? I want to ask her, *Who?*

———

Her dinner with the architect was a quiet affair, as she describes it. *No word was spoken—none could be—and nothing could be heard but an occasional fumble of silverware on china or teeth and the soft sounds of food consumption, not to say digestion.*

———

Was it possible that their relationship simply existed without a name? We commit so many errors in naming something. The act of naming is a lie, uncoupling the named thing from its physicality, from its vulnerability to gravity and time and weathering. A name can only ever allude to, suggest, trace the circumference of the thing to which it refers: ultimately, the word leaves the absence of or, worse, a longing for the thing named.

On trying to answer a question during the trial, one that he had a hard time answering, the architect would simply say,
I cannot say that. I think everything.

———

What did I want at this time? Not a spouse or a boyfriend. Not a person to live with. Not even a person necessarily to speak to every day. Not a roommate.

The proximity to someone brilliant, who would occasionally drink with me and tell me bad jokes. Someone who might also want to live in this glass house and occupy it only on the days that I did not.

If I occupy a relationship with no name, just as she did—her relationship with the architect had no name, no coherent category—then perhaps I would reach another kind of liminal door, another way to access her, to dwell in the same space.

Is that what she wanted?

———

In Yevgeny Zamyatin's *We*, the Russian novelist imagines the twenty-sixth century as a dystopian world in which everything is made of glass. People are given identifying numbers, not names, and sex is a social function—the only reason that one may close their curtains during the day, for the one allotted hour with the person registered to them through the great bureaucratic system.

In the absence of her clarity about *who* in her memoirs, I begin to research and imagine other scenarios of lovers and glass. It gets me nowhere specific, not to any particular answers, but to a thousand different possibilities.

Glass offers both hypervisibility and hyper-obscurity—reflections mapped over reflections. Imagine two people in a chair in a living room. They are next to a large window on a second floor, and as they make love, their images are reflected in this window. They can watch themselves. A man on the sidewalk below walks back and forth to try to get a better view.

They notice this, but they ignore it.

The architect himself referred to these mysterious failures as unknowable, impossible to predict, to the point that his excuse becomes a refrain when he defends the glass house on trial: *because of the glass house, because of the glass there are difficult problems no architect knows.* When pressed by the cross-examining attorney for more specifics, he gives one example:

Q: *Such as?*
A: *The sun's influence on the house.*
Q: *The sun?*
A: *[No.] The influence of the sun.*

9.

What Roland Barthes writes: *The love story (the "episode," the "adventure")
is the tribute the lover must pay to the world in order to be reconciled with it.*

I am sitting in my office with the lights off as the afternoon burns away
outside—summer has returned, though it is fall. The landline rings. There
is a man on the other end and he tells me there are eighteen pages missing
from Edith's memoirs. He's writing a film script that's entirely based on the
premise that she and the architect were lovers, which is the story he believes
is contained in these missing pages. I ask him how he can prove this, and
he says something about frayed edges in one of her notebooks. He wants
me to offer an explanation, as if all women can explain the actions of all
other women. I hang up.

One of the reasons Edith is suspected of being the architect's lover is
that they didn't design and build the house quickly. The absent pauses in
building this house punctuate what should have been a fairly straightfor-
ward process and yet took five years, from 1946 to 1951. These pauses in
production are later described by an architect who worked in this office as
a *loving thing.*

What is it about love that allows for such pauses, for *long periods between
action?*

She reads Ortega y Gasset, is obsessed with his description of the abyss. I
do not know if she reads his other books, if she has come across this passage
in *On Love* in which he argues that love takes time because it is *a constant
state of migration toward the object of our affection.* Or in the simple words
of Saint Augustine, *my love is my weight; where it goes, I go.*

Since desire is a move toward acquisition, toward the desired object
becoming a part of oneself, *desire automatically dies when it is fulfilled; it
ends with satisfaction. Love, on the other hand, is eternally unsatisfied.* It is in
eternal transit.

At least, this is the theory.

―――――

This thing shifts in my hands, like glass. It is a slow-moving liquid on
the cusp of becoming something else.

My pregnant friend and I draw shapes over and over with white chalk on
the floor of my apartment, imagining a glass wall that becomes pregnant,
a glass sheet that encounters and consumes the world. We use my credit

card to pay a man thousands of dollars to blow a series of glass bubbles into the shapes that we've drawn. We bring a wooden mold with us to get some of the hard edges of the shapes we want and the hot glass ignites it, starting a fire in the studio. The gaffer opens all the doors to clear the smoke and gives us paddles covered in layers of charred, ashy newspaper to use to shape the bubbles instead. My friend, whose pregnant belly bubble has been attracting strangers for months, who slaps away their hands, volunteers to press the bubbles. Ashy traces of newspaper are set on fire as she works, become airborne, and dance around her, extinguishing in her dark hair. Her husband stands back, watching, looking exhausted.

We get comfortable enough with the process that we take turns forcing our own breath into the body of glass at the end of the long metal tube, the gaffer begging us not to breathe in by accident, not to singe our lungs.

Some of the bubbles burst, or fail, or parts are broken off and they drop onto the floor. I scoop a few ends into my pocket when we are leaving, even though when I had been caught doing this before, the gaffer told me that the glass was likely to explode as it cooled and slapped it out of my hand.

The whole surface of my desk is covered in what I stole, the glass lips that had connected the bubbles to the pipes. I move the fragments of the lips of the bubbles to the windowsill—gaping, transparent mouths, perpetually empty.

———

I learn that it is possible that the frayed edges in her notebooks are all that are left of pages that were pulled out by concerned friends after she died. Alice T. Friedman, the historian who began this work before I did, was the first to see Edith's notebooks in bags in her family's garage and gently suggested to her nephew that they belonged in an archive or library.

Some chapters of Edith's memoirs are labeled in her own hand—Chapter One, Chapter Two—other chapters appear to be labeled in someone else's hand, a distinction that suggests either an actual renumbering or that I am paranoid. And yet, women slip through, are not erased from these pages. M.G.P., from the Castine photograph, is Mary G. Porter, who would have been known to her friends as Polly Porter. Edith remembers her *as a beautiful girl in a white riding habit astride of her black horse, galloping over the roads and fields.*

In her memoirs, Edith quotes (or invents) an unknown source that seems to stand in as the disembodied voice of the social mores of this rich enclave of Maine: *"Nobody could understand why Miss Porter never married, what with all the young men who came to visit at the Moss Acre. But she didn't and finally the old people died and then Polly went overseas in the First World War and when she came back again Miss Dewson was with her and since then they've always been together. There's folks that don't like Miss Dewson but then there's no accounting for people and perhaps Miss Porter's better off this way. But you should have seen her all in white, galloping on that black horse!"*

". . . and finally the old people died."

In this photograph, she is M.G.P., not Polly or Miss Porter. Her hair is loosely pinned up, a white flower behind her right ear, her collared white dress covered with a dark cardigan, her knee up and hands clasped over it, looking at her partner, Molly Dewson—the American feminist and prominent women's suffrage activist—who is taking this photograph. Edith, who summered at Gray Gables, her aunt's house in Castine, would likely have met Polly there and been familiar with her family's seasonal home, Moss Acre. The six women clustered on these rocks in coastal Maine (and one behind the camera) represent the first generation of educated (and privileged) white American women who had the money and power to embrace their sexuality, to question the institution of marriage, to reject the structures handed to them, to build new ones.

But in Edith's memoirs, we get only a shadow of recognition of Porter's life with Dewson in this offhand phrase: *perhaps Miss Porter's "better off this way. But you should have seen her."*

This way. In an iconic photograph of Molly and Polly, they wear matching fur coats, walking a very fluffy, almost bearlike dog in Van Cortlandt Park in the Bronx in 1925. They are radiant together. Edith would visit them at their home in New York, an apartment cooperative where they lived in the winters. It was full of unmarried women who were like-minded in political leanings, who lived in units alone, or in couples.

The subjects they discussed during visits and picnics are described in Edith's memoirs as *social and political issues*. Very little else is expressed, and she does not give her own opinions, nor does she reveal her relationship with M.G.P., Molly Dewson, or any of the other women in her memoirs in a way that would allow us to draw any specific conclusions. We could read Edith's relative silence, her omission, in many ways.

Edith's memoirs are written at the end of her life, decades after this photograph is taken, and they are written for an audience, though that imagined audience remains unknown. Her education took place under circumstances in which she was one of the "quota of four" women admitted into her graduating class at Northwestern University Medical School, when working women were seen to erode the American family. In the 1930s, the *New York Times* reported in front-page news that women *suffering from masculine psychological states* (loving women) could be cured by having one of their adrenal glands removed, a correction that would fix their *aversion to marriage*. The majority of her career as a doctor, medical researcher, and professor took place during the Lavender Scare, from the late 1940s into the 1960s, during which time anyone even socializing with someone "suspected" of being gay (at the time they used the term "homosexual") made them "guilty" by association. The government, under the sway of Senator Joseph McCarthy's hysteria, regularly and procedurally harassed and fired people suspected of being gay, justified by the U.S. Senate who claimed that they exhibited a *weakness of their moral fiber*. Perhaps the muscle memory of silencing was still present as she wrote her memoirs. Perhaps the friction between self and performance of self (for survival) eroded her ability to give language to this world or the desire to do so.

And yet, in this photograph of women in Castine, nothing is censored: there is joy, no self-consciousness, just camaraderie. It is the only photograph I have ever seen of Edith in which she looks fully relaxed, unspooled, almost unrecognizably secure in herself among these women.

———

When Edith and Katharine Butler (not yet Hathaway) spend a winter together in Paris, in what she describes in her memoirs as *squalid studio rooms on the Left Bank*, Edith reflects that

> we used to drink hot chocolate with brioches at the Coupole in the late afternoon while the rain streamed down outside, and talk about Toshihiko and about life, and all our thoughts and experiences. "Like Miss Furr and Miss Skeene who went to Paris to be gay," Katharine would say, and we would laugh and laugh.

Gertrude Stein's story "Miss Furr and Miss Skeene" appeared in the July 1923 edition of *Vanity Fair*, a few years before Edith and Katharine were in Paris. It begins:

Helen Furr had quite a pleasant home. Mrs. Furr was quite a pleasant woman. Mr. Furr was quite a pleasant man. Helen Furr had quite a pleasant voice, a voice quite worth cultivating. She did not mind working. She worked to cultivate her voice. She did not find it gay living in the same place where she had always been living. She went to a place where some were cultivating something, voices and other things needing cultivating. She met Georgine Skeene there who was cultivating her voice which some thought was quite a pleasant one. Helen Furr and Georgine Skeene lived together then.

The story goes on to repeat the word "gay" over and over, 132 times by my count. But Stein argued *that there is no such thing as repetition.* She would call this *insistence.* To Stein, portraying the *insistence* of a subject invoked their presence, set them in motion across time. Mrs. Furr becomes Miss Furr, Miss Furr and Miss Skeene are gay, they live together, and eventually, they live apart. The meaning of *gay* transforms throughout the piece, and after several repetitions it becomes clear that it describes Miss Furr and Miss Skeene's relationship—*they were quite regularly gay there, Helen Furr and Georgine Skeene, they were regularly gay there where they were gay. They were so very regularly gay. To be regularly gay was to do every day the gay thing that they did every day.*

Vanity Fair gave the story this tag line: *The Tale of Two Young Ladies Who Were Gay Together and How One Left the Other Behind.* A paragraph introducing the story states that *the style, though queer, is exactly suited to the subject.* In the United States, by around 1914, *queer* was a derogatory adjective when used outside of, but not within, the queer community. No doubt, there was little ambiguity about Gertrude Stein's text, as Stein herself was openly gay and had been in a committed relationship with Alice B. Toklas since 1907.

In her memoirs, Edith pretends to know none of this, writing, *I do not remember now, and probably did not then, how gay Gertrude Stein's characters were in Paris.* She describes what drove Miss Furr and Miss Skeene to Paris, to be gay, as *privations.* In contrast, she writes, Katharine's motivations *were categorical and profound, but the skies of Paris dripped nothing but drops of sordidness and vice.*

During this time, Katharine wrote and drew and was visited by her former lover and friend, a Japanese painter, Toshihiko. It was not *privations,* in the end, that drove Katharine out of Paris but what Toshihiko was turning her into: *a listener, a consoler, simply a woman; and this mood is utterly contrary to creative mood*, she complained. She decamps to Haute-Savoie for the spring to visit a friend—a former showgirl—who is in a sanatorium being treated for tuberculosis. Finding the patients boring, they instead rent a house with some construction workers until the arrangement dissolves into what Katharine describes as a *murky tangle of deception*, and she returns to Maine.

———

Katharine Butler Hathaway writes a letter to a friend on June 30, 1942, just a few years after Edith graduates medical school but years before she meets the architect:

> *Edith has written to me. . . . There was a guarded secret—a love affair. Heavens—I hope she will be discreet + very wary or the wolves will be after her + she'll be ruined.*

Who is this living, breathing Edith? What wolves and why?

———

To try to label Edith would be a violence that I refuse to enact.

She would, anyway, resist it. The one man who followed her to Italy at the end of her life, who offered to act as her literary executor, who said he would take her papers with him, and revise them to show a *reconciliation between a great architect and a great client*—she laughed at him. *It was the height of ghoulishness*, she writes in a letter to her sister, who also rarely appears in the memoirs except in childhood.

What kind of burial is language anyway?

10.

All week, men have been emailing me images of women who are not Edith. They become angry and incredulous when I reject their insistence that they are helping me research. One man emails me a photograph of a woman lying prone on her daybed, her arm resting over her face, a gesture of voluptuous and almost comical defeat. I can tell it's not Edith—too much curve to the hip, a very strong nose, and a delicate blouse, one with lace at the collar.

This isn't the woman I'm writing about, I respond.

No, you're wrong, he argues, but I don't read the paragraph.

FIGURE 9. Jenny Huebner Geering, Edith Farnsworth House, c. 1954.

This is a photograph I have also seen in her archive, one of few images in her collection that shows a person in the glass house. Many historians insist this is her. The person it most looks like, to me, is the architect's then-girlfriend, Lora Marx, the Chicago-based sculptor—the same strong nose, the same style of dress, and short fingernails: when I zoom in, I see something dark embedded just under her nails, the characteristic hands of an artist who may have worked with a dye or a challenging material. I love this photograph for the confusion it sows and have always wondered if she included it in her collection for that purpose.

As much as I want this reclining woman to be Lora Marx, I eventually learn that she is a Swiss pianist, Jenny Huebner Geering. Every Friday evening, from the mid-1940s to the early 1950s, Geering hosted a chamber orchestra in her apartment near Lake Michigan. Edith attended these, likely because her colleague at Passavant Hospital, Dr. Verbruggen, was an occasional cellist in Geering's living room orchestras. She and Edith became such close friends that when Geering underwent surgery at Passavant Hospital and began to hallucinate from the medication her physicians prescribed, Edith sneaked her out of the hospital wrapped up in a fur coat and drove her home to her family. Her son Stephen says he can still see the image of his mother enveloped in fur as Edith walked her into their house.

———

But the photograph that locates her, for me, is her graduation portrait. She has just completed medical school. In it, something is happening that is beyond language. It is best described in a letter written by a woman who remembered her from this time:

sumac of cheek and strangely golden of both spirit and hair

I recall that this letter was in the first folder of the first box of her archive, preceding almost all else. It took all of my power not to slip it into my jacket.

FIGURE 10. Edith Farnsworth, 1938.

This is the only image I have of her in which she is still. In almost all the other photographs of Edith that I find, she is in action: gardening, picnicking, holding a large wicker basket, lighting a cigarette. In the cigarette photograph, there is another woman sitting next to her: the wife or girlfriend of one of the young architects in Mies's office. One day, frustrated with historians' tendency to misidentify her, I hold up my copy of it and take off this other woman's head with a hole puncher. It is a circle of light whenever I lift the photograph off my desk.

What Jae Emerling writes—that within every photograph, there is some ecstatic moment that dismantles the chronology, that smashes the distance between the viewer and the image: *what wounds us interrupts our studious reading.*

A wound: I see, I feel, hence I notice, I observe, I think.

———

In the archives of famous men, women often appear in fragments, unidentified, misidentified, or conflated with other women. This happens with regularity in the emails people send me as I write this book; women who are younger than her are mistaken for Edith, women who, after further research, are often labeled as *girlfriend of* _____ or *wife of* _____ or, worse, a series of initials. All of them tethered to historical record by a man, a leash that chokes while it holds them from being swept into the abyss of time, a dark and hungry hole.

But men are also a reason that women disappear. Like the architect's secretary, who spoke both English and German, who looked, as the man being interviewed put it, *thin and nervous.*

A longish face, architectural historian Kevin Harrington offers, to soften words he probably senses are coming next.

She was fixated on the architect, the man tells Harrington; it was *unmanageable in her own mind,* she *left in kind of a huff, just disappeared.*

She simply disappeared.

It was a very strange . . . disappearance of a woman.

He says this as if it makes sense. As if women fixate on men until they cannot function, and then, with nothing mooring them to reality or to this earthly plane, they vanish, float away.

Institutional imaginations do not make the same mistake with men. The architect was introduced to American audiences with a retrospective of his work at the Museum of Modern Art in 1947. Her house is exhibited here, introduced to the world in the form of a model. In fact, every building the architect has ever designed up to this date is here in this exhibition—even the ones that have already been destroyed. Each building is depicted in photographs blown up to such large proportions that they stop being photographs and start to be buildings again. They swallow the museum walls.

The buildings have no humans in them, but they often contain sculptures of stone women. The stone women do not yet know that they might be destroyed along with the buildings they occupied, or that they might be taken into storage, or even become part of a museum collection somewhere. At the center of this exhibition is a life-size photograph of the architect's Barcelona Pavilion, built in 1929. The photograph is so large that the wall disintegrates; it is as if we can walk into it. The vanishing point in the perspective of this photograph is the navel of George Kolbe's sculpture of *Dawn*, a young woman whose hands are drawn up over her head to fend off the glancing blows of an imaginary sun.

In the next room of this retrospective exhibition, a photographic repro-duction of the Tugendhat House in Brno, Czech Republic, 1930, swallows up yet another wall. In this photograph, a woman's head and nude torso, carved from white marble with stumps for arms and legs, turns to face the camera. She's been placed on a pedestal and is a striking contrast to the black marble wall behind her. The architect stands in the museum with his back to this photograph, his back to her, to the whole house depicted behind him. A thin, chrome-plated column is the only visible structural element of this house, twinned in the mirrored wall behind it and in the perfectly reflective surface of a glass table in the foreground. The column disappears into the white ceiling above it, which matches exactly the white of museum walls, the same white as the IKEA desk beneath my laptop. There is no space between the future, the present, or the past. The architect stands with his left hand tucked away in his pocket, a cigar dangling from his right. And not quite cut from the photograph, her house, on the blurry periphery of this image—its foam trees floating around the model of the glass house like a gray fog.

The architect's first suggestion of a glass house is included in the catalog for this exhibition: a collaboration with Lilly Reich, *Glasraum*, created for an exposition on housing in Stuttgart, Germany, in 1927. It was comprised of a study, living room, and dining room, with the sculpture of a legless,

FIGURE 11. Ludwig Mies van der Rohe with Farnsworth House model.

armless woman by Wilhelm Lehmbruck trapped inside one of its patios. Interchangeable glass houses, interchangeable women.

In a photograph that seems almost accidental at first glance, the model of Edith's glass house sits on a pedestal. The architect leans into this image— some historical accounts will say he is examining it like a proud father examines a newborn. I see him craning over the edge of the model, his head hovering beside the carved-foam trees, peering into the bedroom as if he were trying not to be seen, watching.

11.

The glass bubbles I made with my pregnant friend are being polished by a man who slices them apart with a diamond-studded saw, opening each one like a body to reveal the soft, continuous folds of glass, so human and, when polished, so soft to the touch. I run my fingertips over one of them in his shop. *It can't cut you*, he says, *no teeth*.

My friend's body is swelling, and she is pissed off. Winter in Portland is cold, perpetually wet. We squat in an unheated garage we borrowed from a friend, laminating wood veneer to the edges of slender pedestals we have built. We work so long that my back cramps and I rock back on my heels to rest, but she will not stop working, her body furious with child.

As my friend grows heavier, I grow lighter, unmoored to reality, sometimes confused, counting down the days until I apply for tenure, terrified it will not have been enough, unsure how I will survive, financially, how I will pay student loans, how I will pay rent, how I will eat.

———

The architect hesitated at first to build her house because he didn't believe she could afford it. Who knows what about her signaled this concern. *I would never cheapen something to build it*, he tells her, the woman who will inherit two lumber companies.

Alfred Caldwell, a young man who had been hired to draw the house, was sitting next to her in the architect's living room during this conversation. Caldwell looked at her, and she looked back at him. He believed that the architect had just refused to design the house because she did not have the money.

———

I write the check for rent and slide it through the slot in the door downstairs, feed the room in the basement that takes the money. I eat sardines over rice.

———

In a letter she writes to the architect, she makes it very clear that she is *not willing* to spend everything she has to make the house. She did not want to be *on the town*, as she puts it, should the expenses become astronomical or should she lose her job for any reason. Then he suggests that instead of a concrete floor for the house, they order Roman travertine. She agrees.

The idea of debt is the idea of indiscriminate spending, the idea that the poor have no concept of how money works. But I am deeply indebted, and I remember everything that I have spent money on. I still remember the taste of the ricotta in a dish I ordered in Ottawa years ago on a research trip; I remember the two glasses of wine I consumed, eating alone at the bar, the decadence of owing nobody my attention, the awareness that I was already tipsy but could get drunk, the deep smell of good red wine, a smell like essentialized earth in my glass, even the way the snow fell outside, visible from where I ate but so far away as to be something to watch, not something to consider. There was a man screaming on the sidewalk outside, screaming until someone came along and made him silent. I knew what he was screaming about, have lived it, am living it, but evading it because of the privilege and burden of debt. The extravagant red coat, the boots that glide over my knee. With every expense, fleecing an animal called my future.

————

Glass, in general, is the enemy of secrets. It is also the enemy of possession, writes Walter Benjamin, complaining about the architect and his contemporaries. Those who would design glass rooms have already devoured everything, he writes, both people and culture, and they long, at last (and exhausted) to free themselves of any human experience.

Just a few years earlier than this, the architect would underline the following warning from Siegfried Ebeling in a German book from 1926, *Der Raum als Membran*. It will not be translated into English by another author until 2014, too late to do anyone any good, buried under a few of my credit card statements: *It is the symptom of a dying culture that a populace produces more than it can use, that it whips its spirit harder than is good for it, that it anticipates needs that it itself does not have.*

————

When she discovers that costs for the elements of the house have skyrocketed, invoices of already ordered steel for the structure and travertine marble for the floor (inside and out) washing ashore on her desk, she is furious. He sends her furniture for the house as a peace offering. She rejects it. I try not to read into the theory that the furniture he sent is designed on the proportions of his own body—so wide, so thick, so low to the ground. His body, in multiples, threatening to populate her house.

There are other theories that this interruption meant the end of a line of furniture he was designing specifically for her house. The only historical reference to this furniture exists in an interview with Myron Goldsmith, the young project architect. Goldsmith says that the architect had intended for the glass house to contain furniture upholstered in hides with the hair still on them. The architect was obsessed with hides, with Indigenous forms of architecture as he understood them, particularly what he called an "Eskimo villa," a hut made of fur and bones. *Now I take you into the night and ice,* he would announce in his lectures.

———

In my family, hides are passed down from generation to generation. After my great-aunt's husband was shot to death during the drunken card game, she had photographs of herself taken in which she posed with her hunting rifle. Every animal she loved she had sewn into a coat or an accessory after their death.

When I am home during a winter break from teaching, I wear her pony coat for a long walk. I stagger under the weight of it as I cross a snow-covered field, moving in slow, wide circles until my legs collapse under me, wondering as I sink to the ground if I'd be mistaken for an animal, having been out of Nebraska for too long to remember which hunting season it could be.

———

If we were to go to the house together, I could stand in the bare spot where she slept, on the floor between a glass wall and the fireplace. And in that empty space is a whole essay on the minimalism of wealth, which is so different than the minimalism of poverty.

The first time I read that essay was as a child, when our family moved into my uncle's empty, beautiful mansion for a year. He had asked us to house-sit while he moved his family to London, but my aunt, aware that poverty oozes, that it stains, that it rubs its greasy fingers into expensive upholstery, had their furniture placed in storage. We moved our faded things into the house, sat on couches and beds as if they were life rafts in an otherwise vast ocean of space.

Years later, my mother would drive across the river between the state she grew up in and the state I grew up in, the unsecured boxes in the back of our truck bouncing, generations of glass heirlooms shattering behind her so that when she got home, we just took the boxes to the curb for recycling and never spoke of how she freed me of these things.

———

She would later refer to him as a *peasant.*

He, in turn, would show up while the house was being constructed just to sit in a blue canvas chair. He would approve or disapprove of slabs of marble intended for the floors as the men building the house walked by in single file, holding them. These slabs of marble are two feet long by almost three feet wide and over an inch thick: I cannot imagine a human carrying one. As each man marched by, slab of marble in hand, the architect would gesture to indicate whether the slab was acceptable or not. Only the finest for his house.

———

You know where she got the money, right? Against my better judgment, I answer my office phone, and it's the same man, the one making the movie about the architect-client romance. He begins talking and loops endlessly around a subject he calls her *marital failure*, that her parents were disappointed in her for not marrying, and this is why she had to wait for an inheritance from her aunt to be able to afford to build her house, an inheritance that represented only a fraction of the overall cost. When I begin to speak, he says, *call anytime you want more information about her*. I hang up without saying goodbye and sit in the quiet, cool dark of my office.

At the end of the summer, my tenure package is due. It would allow me, for the first time in my adult life, some financial stability: the possibility of paying off student loan debt, the possibility of staying in one place, not moving again to another town, another job, as I had done through my mid-twenties and thirties while everybody I knew was beginning a life. I kept beginning lives and throwing them away. There were conditions in my life that were more real than the people around me: the necessity of paying off an extraordinary heap of student loans, the gentrification and rising cost of rent that eroded the ground beneath my feet, the lives I had not lived because I broke them off and moved, let them pile up behind me.

———

When she lent the architect a copy of Erwin Schrödinger's *What Is Life?* he returned it to her, furious, a few days later. *I want to know what I have to expect after death,* he said. He refused to believe that he was mortal, that his fate was, as he put it, *the same as the snowflakes on the window, the salt crystals on the dinner table.*

Jesus, what story do you want? I ask out loud, touching my bald spot. I have begun to accept that nothing grows here, and the tips of my fingers graze over it as I worry it smooth.

She was his physician, a role she performed for him at no cost. *We tried,* she writes, in the margin of a notebook. *We tried to shield him from the intolerable apprehension of his own extinction.*

In place of death, in his own notes, the architect would write "eternal life." *And yet man also has the needs of his soul, which can never be satisfied by merely making sure that he does not get stuck in his walls.*
And *silence. Silence.*

Have I mentioned his desperation yet? How desperately he needed to build? That by the time she hired him to design her house, he had been in the United States since 1937, about ten years, and had still not built a house?

What might he have said, or promised, to get her to agree to trust him to build this?

Why this desperation to scratch the earth, to leave a mess?

A death expert on the radio says that humans are the only creatures aware that they will die. We are aware of this fact almost every single day of our lives. *It's why we do everything*, she explains.

Is this why he did not choose to live in glass? Instead, he lived on the third floor of a typical brick apartment building in Chicago from which he could see his glass towers.

———

Even someone believing in eternal life would have to accept that we go through a physical transformation when we die. Or does their fruit not rot on the counter?

12.

The first night that she sleeps on the floor of the house, suspended above the floodplain, is December 31, 1950, the cusp of the second half of the twentieth century. A century in which it becomes clear, with the development of the nuclear bomb, that what will almost certainly end the world is humans. She sleeps in a glass house in a country that holds that particular world-destroying power. Perhaps it's worth knowing that this American glass house is not yet complete and that she slept in it anyway: *spots and strokes of white paint* on the glass, no curtains, one bare, sixty-watt bulb illuminating the white, frozen plains that stretch out in every direction. The keys do not yet belong to her.

She receives one phone call that evening from a neighbor, begging her to vacate the house: *you don't know how quick the river can rise.*

She describes this as *an uneasy night, partly from the exposure provided by the uncurtained glass walls and partly from the ^ fear of [the architect's] implacable intentions.*

" ^ " means I must follow the blue line underneath this sentence across the gutter of the spread and onto the left side where on an otherwise empty page she writes one word she has tethered to the others:

^ *dread.*

———

Where does the tethered dread belong? Right next to my palpating heart.

What do I do to untether? I tear my mind out of my body and I work.

———

My brain believes it controls my body, but my body is the one that throws on the brakes.

One morning, at yet another conference hotel, it is a pain in my chest so intense that I drop onto the bed, fully clothed, expecting to die. I wait. Death never comes.

During this conference, it becomes difficult to distinguish the shudder of my heart from the shudder of the hotel itself, the building under an ambitious amount of construction. The walls shake all day as if we are being bombed. Fresh slips of over-Xeroxed paper saying *bear with us!* in blurry lettering appear on the pillows every time I come back to my room, the bed perpetually unmade, the air grimy with construction dust.

———

I learn that for $10,000, I can take a leave of absence from my department for ten weeks—a period during which I might be able to focus on research, to rest, to temporarily assuage the anxiety that threatens to take my body apart.

When the grant arrives, I give the funds to my department chair. It's a form of escape, like any material pleasure—money, luxury goods, sex—to avoid thinking about the way in which my time is being frittered away, teaching without a moment to breathe, knowing that at the end of every day, I have lost something I can never regain.

The search for evidence of the history of a love affair between the architect and client is escapist, but I am too invested to stop. What Roland Barthes writes—*History is hysterical: it is constituted only if we consider it, only if we look at it—and in order to look at it, we must be excluded from it.* I want to stand outside of time to look at this history.

With this grant, I should have paid myself: I should have purchased equipment or books, but I buy space instead. I space myself out.

I move to Chicago, again, make it my fixed point and, from here, live everywhere. I decide to begin again, begin in the city where they met. I want to trace the human imprint of the history I've read, to find the historian who wrote that she was *no beauty, equine in feature,* that she *expected the architect to go along with the house,* the one who published the passport photograph of her when she is in her eighties next to this passage, as if it is proof that she is unlovable or simply to humiliate her. Her face is contorted in this photograph, as if she knows; one eye squints hard.

Through a quick online search, I find this historian's email address and discover he is still affiliated with a college in a wealthy Chicago suburb. I fire off an email so that I can say that I did it, I tried to reach out. I am shocked when I hear the muffled *ping* from my coat jacket. He invites me to lunch at the Arts Club.

We both order the soup. When I press him to explain why he spent so many pages of the architect's biography nursing the theory that she was vengeful, in love with the architect, hired him from obsession and then sued him out of rage after he'd moved on romantically, he looks at me with a blank expression. *Every writer is vulnerable.*

Vulnerable to what? He shrugs again. *Every writer needs a story.*

He clears his throat, and lunch is over.

———

After this, I go into a gallery and watch, slide by slide, projected images of a small, wooden, steam-powered boat named *Dignity* being chopped to pieces by axe-wielding passengers who feed the chunks into *Dignity's* wood-burning stove. This fuels the boat as it tries to cross Scotland's Loch Long.

I watch until *Dignity* sinks and its debris floats on the surface of the water. I watch as the passengers swim away, out of frame, leaving a projection of the surface of the water, a small square of light and motion in an otherwise vast sea of darkness.

13.

I had hoped to buy space. What I have purchased is time. This may be the last time that I will be able to afford to spend weeks in her archive. I am in no rush because it is fall, and nobody is doing research here anymore. A retired man at a corner table sifts through papers at a retired rate. Nobody bangs on the glass with their fists to be let in, and at times, nobody is even present to observe us, to watch us as we work.

I hold each document with my bare hands, one piece at a time, lingering over the tangential ones that I have previously ignored: each poem, each translation, each page of her journal, each photograph that she took. Instead of reading, I photograph everything. I even photograph the boxes that contain the documents, their dull blue, their reinforced metal edges. Exposure by exposure, I replicate her archive.

I photograph a poem that she translated both for the poem itself and for the way that my hand casts a shadow over it, like the shadow of a bird passing overhead, one that is already gone by the time you look up.

———

In the midst of this research, I am becoming known as, alternately, an expert on the glass house and an expert on the architect's sex life. Although neither of these is the truth, I am entertained by the failure of institutions to imagine or explain a history in which a woman's life is central.

I give a lecture in Venice, and among the questions that I am asked about this research is whether the architect was a "sex freak." This question arrives before dawn the morning after the lecture, in the dark underbelly of a water taxi to the airport that I share with a Dutch architect. And into the darkness, I answer, *I don't know.* The trapped air begins to turn around us.

The university that had organized this week of events put me up in a hotel on a canal, rooms swarming with mosquitoes.

That afternoon, face swollen with mosquito bites, in a brick building called the Arsenale that is almost a thousand years old, where Venice once mass-produced ships at a rate of nearly one per day, I spoke to an audience of mostly students about the project of tracing this woman's history. I was asked, *How will it end?* And I didn't have an answer. *I don't know that it will,* I responded. There was an awkward silence and then some confused clapping.

Yes, yes, said the Dutch architect. He squeezed my arm all the way to the restaurant where we had lunch with rich people from whom the university was trying to extract donations. *THIS is the end of modernism; it dies like THIS*, he said, and he offered to write the introduction to the book that I had not even begun, the book I was only living, not yet writing. *What is THIS*, I began to ask but stopped, because as we walked I could feel the city move under my feet. I felt it rise and fall. I felt it breathe, and it destroyed all the language inside of me.

————

Is the world as it presents itself bearable to man?
Is it worthy of man or too lowly?
Does it offer room for the highest form of human dignity?
Can it be shaped so as to be worthwhile to live in?

In Chicago, on an unknown date and occasion, the architect gave this lecture, written across nineteen sheets of paper. He asked these questions in the middle of the lecture. He did not attempt to answer them. Instead, he said, *These are questions of immense weight. One can quickly affirm them and quickly negate them, and one has done that.*

————

She keeps her own list of problems associated with the house:

Problems   flood waters
        footings, roofing, utilities, doors, partitions, glass,
        personnel

visitors

There were problems. Did she know the questions to ask? These included the fact that lighting a fire in the hearth in the hermetically sealed house caused interior negative pressure—the outside air moved in, blowing out the fire. To keep the fire burning, she opened the door. The fireplace was designed to be a minimal presence: when she first moved in, before the architect designed andirons for it, the logs burned directly on the floor. From time to time, a burning log would roll across the room.

During these weeks in Illinois, I avoid the house entirely. I suspend myself in the space and time before its full realization.

I reach out to other eminent historians. I reach one who calls me "dear," who tells me that the client and the architect were indeed intimates and that the lack of evidence is itself evidence; that, as intimates, the space between them was short, a shallow chasm, and like all shallow chasms, it contained a dearth of communication. *My dear, they were simply too close to one another to leave any traces of their relationship.*

I call the Library of Congress and ask for every love letter from the architect to all the women with whom he was involved. There are only two that I know of—Lora Marx, the sculptor in Chicago, and Mary Callery, the sculptor in New York. He seemed to float between the two freely.

At the Library of Congress, they can find only his General Office files in which correspondence with the New York sculptor concerns artwork that he had given her or that she had given him and requests for permission to lend the works to exhibitions.

This takes place years after the completion of the glass house.

On April 5, 1957, Mary Callery writes, *Do let me know when you are next in town.*

And on December 15, 1963, *I hear vaguely of your news, but would love to know how you really are.*

She should consider herself lucky. Lora Marx receives correspondence from the architect's secretary, Connie, that he had sent her a card on August 13, 1953, saying, *I shall be back August 27 if everything goes as planned*—did they not have telephones? There are letters in 1955 concerning an air conditioner installed at Marx's apartment and two in 1956 and 1957 concerning the architect's application for a 1957 and 1958 state license for his Oldsmobile.

This cannot possibly be all of their correspondence, but it's all that history allows us to access.

————

In her memoirs, there is no reference to a lover.

————

Under oath, Mies would be asked to explain the nature of their relationship.

Q: *Were you good friends, close friends?*
A: *Yes, we were.*

————

I spend the other half of each week, when I am not in her archive, devoted to the words and ideas of historians and to authorities of the past, the people who were alive when she was. I spend hours at the Regenstein Library on the campus of the University of Chicago. The library's reading room is a large glass bubble. On one desk, I have collected a copy of every book that references her. Each tells a love story in the same way: she is a woman who hired the architect because she was in love with him, and when the love affair ended, she conspired to sue him, to trash his reputation. Not even the most basic facts are correct: the fact that he sued her first, trying to extract more money from her for fees that they'd never agreed to (he wanted to be paid for his work as an architect and as a general contractor, having hired himself to subcontract out the work), the fact that she countersued him because the costs for the house had spiraled out of control, the price for the structure an always-moving target. No mention of the lien he put on the house to try to force her out of it, to keep it for himself. Instead, each version of this history is a B-movie plot starring a hysterical woman and a heroic architect. The adherence to a narrative structure is strong—each contains a footnote reaching back to the origin, the man who told me that *every writer is vulnerable*. His printed words became a foothold for generations of writers who would quote him.

Hell hath no fury, jokes one historian, suggesting that a woman's anger is, at best, petty and laughable.

————

Exposure by exposure, I return to the Newberry Library. Exposure is the word we use for taking a photograph: exposing film to light, allowing it to—in the case of black-and-white photography—turn invisible silver halide crystals into specks of silver embedded in film. Exposure here means damage—damage that creates an image. Taking a photograph on an iPhone is completely different: it samples light from the world. With enough samples, we believe we have a faithful representation of reality.

Researching a history is the same way: with enough samples interpreted the same way, we believe we have a correct narrative.

I finish documenting the front and back of every single item in her archive. I have no idea yet how they might add up, all of them interpreted into the same proportions, each given a random number generated by my phone, an archive within the ever-growing archive of my own life—her life sandwiched between photographs I'd taken of meals, my purse on the bedspread because the light was just so, a photograph from the window of my Airbnb when I tried to catch the sunset. It didn't quite work, the light tearing through the lens of the camera phone and bursting into pure white in the image, pure nothing.

14.

When I return to Portland, there are new rituals. Late at night, someone's ex-boyfriend will occasionally shatter the front door of the apartment building, a bright explosion of sound as the glass breaks, like applause. And one afternoon, a wall of this same building collapses, sending a shower of bricks all over the sidewalk and parked cars. I stand across the street in the rain with the rest of my neighbors, eating a bowl of soup the firemen had allowed me time to collect from the kitchen. Later, watching the news, I see footage of us huddled on the sidewalk and labeled *evacuees*. The camera pans to the jagged pile of bricks, and a man who is sifting through it to see if there are any bodies underneath. I hold my breath when I realize I do not see the older woman who manages the building.

Something has turned in the world, and even my students are looking for the broken joint. The ground beneath our feet becomes suspicious. What kind of earth is it? Will it liquefy when the earthquake arrives? Why is the entire state of Oregon's fuel supply held in giant, nearly century-old concrete drums on the riverbank of the Willamette? Which hills will collapse, raining down an avalanche of houses? I can see these hills from my car, stopped in traffic along the part of the interstate that is lifted high on concrete columns over the river. Cars, semis, cement mixers, garbage trucks, and school buses, all of us bouncing up and down like birds collected at the end of a long branch.

For a split moment, when the tectonic plates snap, the earth's crust will thin, and gravity will weaken.

Imagine being, for a moment, untethered.

———

At yet another conference, my body affixed a name tag to its front left side, showing the name that my body went by, its institutional affiliation (where my body got the money to be modestly sheltered, fed, and clothed). It moved in and out of conference rooms, carrying a bag with a laptop in it and that rattling bottle of pills that the doctor gave it but that my body rarely took. My body felt no more pain, no more sudden shocks to the chest. My body stood in line for coffee when there were breaks between meetings, holding conversation just long enough to be friendly but not so long as to become familiar with anyone. My body maintained its autonomy, felt like an object among objects, as much an object as the warm porcelain cup my body held between its hands, a cup that didn't belong to my body, that my body could discard on any table, knowing it would disappear, that the encounter would be marked only by the trace of lipstick which would soon be gone, the cup cleaned and put back into rotation for another self-serve coffee banquet. My body got in sync with the timing of all the other bodies, became a part of the human blood coursing through the veins of the corporate conference hotel, found itself in a long conversation with a thin, balding man who held an important position. To extract might mean career death, so my body nodded slowly as if understanding the man, wondering about that space between itself and the man, the space of obligation and attention, wished for a fire or a stroke to break it, and when another man entered this space, the membrane sealing it broke, and my body was able to dislodge and move freely again. It walked into the women's restroom, found an open stall, and it sat down on the toilet. Safely cocooned in dim light, thin aluminum partitions, and the relieved silence of a few other women, my body reached for the phone in its bag.

———

There is a price to being genius-adjacent, and that price is many more hours than it takes to be a genius. The architect may have *crystallized his ideas*, but Myron Goldsmith—or Goldy, as the architect called him—did the structural calculations, sized the members, and hired the subcontractors who ordered the parts and put them all together to create the house. Edith called him *your young man*, told him *your young man is bothering the builders on site who are trying to get their work done.* Goldsmith was there to supervise the work being translated from the drawings into built form. The drawings traveled back and forth with him from Chicago to Plano, from office to rural site, where the land was broken open and dirt spilled out.

It takes particular effort to guard genius, to unburden it from the terrible task of handling the mundane. And perhaps for these reasons, when we meet genius, it can be disappointing. *My dear*, said the famous architectural historian, *you have absolutely perfect posture.* I had been reading this man's work for years and was one of the chosen handful of faculty members who joined him for dinner. I nodded a thank-you but said nothing: at first, I had remained silent because I had not wanted him to know how ordinary

I was. By the end of dinner, I was silent in protest. I had wanted him to be more like his work than he was.

The wives of geniuses must suffer in some even more particular way. The wife of the architectural historian sat silently through dinner, too. She looked exhausted. What versions of her life must she have buried to organize the one she lived around this man who sits in front of me, cutting his steak into smaller and smaller pieces?

There was a string of men like this in her life, genius men.

Mario Corti, violinist. She studies violin with him in Rome from 1924 to 1926. He sees the way she folds her umbrella and chastises her: *A girl who is untidy in the little things in life is likely to be also in the big ones.*

Umberto Barbaro, poet. She spends a few hours a week with him discussing poetry in a bar. She tries to hand him an umbrella as he steps into the rain, and he says, *It always seems absurd to me to go around holding a little thing over one's head.* (This one she calls an "ideal friendship.")

Elis Berven, Swedish radiologist. He inspires her to study medicine after she quits violin and isn't sure what is next: *This is a moment of misgivings for you, but misgivings are often noble. You will find your way—I am very sure of that.*

Dr. Corcoran, who ran an insulin laboratory in Indianapolis and would show up at her door in Chicago from time to time with no warning: *Come over here and give me a kiss! You do love me, don't you, Edie? Come back at once and give me another kiss! You do love me, don't you?* (Corc was affectionate. Corc, to a dog he was injecting with insulin: *You're the most beautiful little research dog in the world. You love me, too, don't you?*)

Mies van der Rohe, architect. The man she hired to build her glass house, whose first words to her are recorded as *I would love to build any kind of house for you.*

Frankland Dark, architect, a man she renames Malcolm Dark in her memoirs, who is present on the day that the sun explodes over the house. In a letter to her, years later, he writes, *My wife died earlier this year.* (Why does this feel suggestive?) And why does it make me gag, the idea that women fill a role for men, die, then must be replaced like a bolt that holds the machine together.

Fellow Atkinson, architect. She code-names him *the second of two Englishmen,* and he pokes at the brushwood fire in the fireplace when she brings him to the glass house. He says, *It would be dreadful if you were not happy here*. I fall in love with her description of the landscape: *cracklings of autumn were muted by a light covering of crystalline white*. He goes out to look for more wood. I cannot remember if he ever returns.

A man named Michael Jaffe, art historian. He leaves flowers and a note. Their dialogue is muddled—I cannot tell who is speaking in her version of events as they unfold on the evening they spent together in the house, so I must rely on her response to those events: *An evening passed in the company of a stranger . . . the trees full of swelling buds—the glass house took on life and became my own home.*

Eugenio Montale, poet. He doesn't appear in her memoirs at all, and he tells her, *You have been—and still are—a marvelous, almost incredible apparition. Write me immediately*, he demands, *and then just every once in a while, if that is not too tiring.*

Each of these men arrives at a particular time in her life, at a moment when the road splits. Each is a point of reference in some shift she is already making. Whether this is out of desire or chance is unclear.

If it seems surprising, ask yourself what choice women have when men are the structure through which all forms of authorship, power, and capital flow.

———

She fucked the poet, laughs a man who is also writing a book on Edith. *In addition to the violin teacher that she studied with in her twenties when she lived in Italy.* I am in the audience for the first public reading of his as-yet unpublished manuscript when he says it, and I almost vomit.

The next day, this man writes to me. He noticed I was present for his talk and asks if we can "compare notes" since he knows I have been researching her for years and has read my articles (though in the lecture he announced that he was the only scholar researching her). He has a hefty advance from a publisher and a deadline. He needs answers. He promises he'll reference me in a footnote if I help him.

I block his email address so he can never reach me again.

Now who's fucked? I laugh.

15.

The world is slippery. And I am wearing the wrong boots, walking in snowbanks between the sheet of ice that is the sidewalk and the sheet of ice that is the street. On the Montréal Metro, I listen to the recorded announce-ments but understand none of the words; I get off the train when the app on my phone indicates that the version of me that is a blue dot is close to the box labeled Canadian Centre for Architecture. This is my last research trip before the semester ends. It feels like running away. Or, at least, I consider running away. I consider pretending that I'm running away.

At a moment in her memoirs that some historians consider "the end," which is not the end but rather the end of one chapter, she describes wish-ing to envelop herself in fabric so that *only a hole is left . . . to look out and the world outside doesn't even know where the hole is. I wish for envelopment because I don't want to be hurt any further,* she writes. She dreads what she calls *the full appearance* and leaves it at that.

———

When I arrive to the Canadian Centre for Architecture, I am directed to a locker room. I watch a man fold his backpack and place it in his locker and then sit down to change into a pair of elegant loafers. I remove my filthy boots and shove them into a locker. I walk to the counter in my black stockings and sign in. The woman at the desk silently hands me a pair of blue cloth booties to wear inside. They taper up at the toe, elfishly.

I find my way through the building's many carpeted hallways, lost but not wanting to ask for help, the booties clearly marking me "other," perhaps confused, perhaps poor. Anyone who has ever been poor knows that the trick to not looking poor is your shoes. I am muted in the cloth slippers, noiseless as I move from room to room: a ghost. I startle a woman coming around the corner with several books; we trade thin smiles.

In the reading room is a stack of materials waiting for me. It will be avail-able for one day. Tomorrow, there will be a new stack. On the third day, the last. I can't complain about the speed with which I will have to work because my access to these materials is a gift. These are documents from the private collection of Mme. Phyllis Lambert. This archive is only acces-sible because Mme. Lambert's father, Samuel Bronfman, had the foresight to export alcohol across the Canadian border into New York during the American Prohibition era and amassed a fortune. He merged his Distillers Corporation Limited with Joseph E. Seagram & Sons to become Seagram, the largest alcohol distilling operation in the world. In 1954, Lambert convinced her father to fire the architects who had already designed his headquarters in New York and to hire Mies instead. He created an elegant glass tower—the glass amber-gray, almost the color of whiskey. In a famous photograph in which they sit discussing his model for this building, she is vibrant, beautiful, wearing pearls, an elegant white shirt, and glasses. She gestures with a pencil. One can almost hear her voice—her mouth is open. Mies looks past her, sleepily.

A colleague connected me to her and assured me that there was perhaps something to be found here in her collection of papers of the man who was genius-adjacent, Myron Goldsmith, who had done all of the calculations for this glass house.

I arrive at the table where I will sit for days. Before I dig into the boxes, I pick up a drawing sitting on top of them, folded over and over as if someone had once carefully rolled it into a tube and it had flattened for decades in a back room. As I open it, dirt tumbles out.

It is a plan of the house. The house is completely empty except for curtain tracks drawn over it, slicing up the otherwise expansive interior into smaller and smaller rooms—an attempt at privacy that never occurred in real life. The date of the drawing is July 18, 1950, meaning that the house was nearly complete, and perhaps when she saw how transparent it was, she demanded a way of enclosing herself. I brush away the dirt, but the cocoon of some insect is stuck to this blue drawing, its fibers holding fast to the paper. Whatever it was has long since hatched, lived, and died elsewhere. I photograph the cocoon carefully, the fibers like the white lines on the blueprint itself.

Here, in this drawing, is her idea of privacy.

And here I am, prying it open.

Here I am, prying my life into hers.

After I take several exposures, I feel a man's hand on my back, hear him asking me to stop photographing. I surrender the drawing for conservation; someone wants to remove the cocoon.

———

I go to sleep in a room I have rented from a young couple in Montréal, a room that is slightly below ground level. In the morning, I wake to a light dust of snow on the pillow and my hair. A window right above my head has been open all night. I fill the bathtub as hot as I can stand. Dog hair floats on the surface of the water. Their dog digs at the space under the bathroom door, nails scratching against stone. I can hear him biting the steamy air that escapes into the hallway as I carefully remove every dog hair from my wet body, one by one.

By the time I arrive at the CCA reading room for my second day, I look as if I belong here. In Montréal, I mostly stay silent since I do not speak French.

Glass, too, holds secrets. When we look at a plan drawing of a glass house, writes Josep Quetglas, the glass might appear to us to be an actual barrier, an enclosure, something like a thin wall. One line indicates the interior, and one indicates the exterior. But in truth, there is no inside or outside to glass. There is just space, unfolding forever, and an invisible wall that our hand hits when we reach out for something that we cannot have.

I am sitting in Madame Lambert's office. I wait for her. It is still snowing. Tomorrow, she is leaving for Paris (this is where she spends Christmas, her assistant explains). I hide my blue-slippered feet under my chair.

When she arrives, it is suddenly and in sweatpants and elegant boots—her outdoor boots, I note silently, black with fur lining the top. She wears a tremendous amount of eyeliner, and her gray hair is arranged in impressive spikes. When she arrives, she asks for cookies, and when the cookies have been arranged on several plates between us, she wants to know why I am here. I tell her that I'm trying to discover any evidence that the architect of the glass house and the client had an affair. She places both hands on the table and tells me to make a chronology. *Everything is revealed by time.* Then she pushes a plate of cookies toward me. *Eat one,* she says, watching. They are small shortbreads, their outsides covered in a glaze of white and dark chocolate that makes me think of seashells. I push an entire cookie into my mouth in one piece and hold it there for a moment, feel it melt. I realize I never want to leave this building. In these spaces, I am an object among objects; I breathe the carefully filtered air, navigate a few rooms in which I encounter other objects that have been curated for me, organized and labeled for my consumption.

As if she knows this, she says, *Have another,* and we watch the snow outside the window. I push my slippered feet further under my chair.

Myron Goldsmith, the young man who was genius-adjacent to the architect, whose papers I sift through, arranged a chronology under duress. One month after work on the house was finished, in April 1951, he left for Europe. He was called back to testify in court just months later, the architect paying for his return flight, because his understanding of the house exceeded that of the architect, who, when asked about the specifics of the cost of the travertine marble floor or the cause of the leaking roof, simply answered, *All of my houses are experimental.*

Part of what made this young man the perfect weapon in court was his fidelity to chronology. He helped the architect create a document I find in today's pile titled IMPORTANT FACTS OF THE FARNSWORTH HOUSE. It is a series of sentences, each one standing alone, and it is written from the perspective of the architect. In it, the architect explains that he would not have built the house except that she *pushed* him, and he describes the gradual increases in the cost of the house as they built it, which are tolerated less and less by Edith until she finally stops speaking to him.

It opens with:

In 1946 when I designed this house for Plano and made the models, I hesitated to start construction because of the difficult conditions in the building field.

Dr. Farnsworth was eager to proceed with construction and in the winter of 1948 and spring of 1949 pushed me very hard.

In spring 1949: *we could not build the house for less than $50,000,* and then

In early June 1949: *we could hold the cost down to about $60,000,* and this remained true in August 1949, and then

In summer of 1950: *Mr. Goldsmith made a new estimate and the cost came to $65,000* and

One evening: I went to her house and told her this and *she was not particularly pleased but there was no strong reaction,* and then

August 1, 1950: we made another estimate for $70,000, and then

August 7, 1950: she wrote a letter, limiting us to this sum, and then by

February 20, 1951: costs amounted to $74,000, which *included about $2,800 worth of items not in the original estimate and usually not included in the construction costs of a house,* which are not explained or described in this document anywhere, and the architect asked Myron Goldsmith to tell Edith. He did.

When the architect *called her a few days later she accused Mr. Goldsmith and me of having known this fact long before on a trip from Plano when she had asked whether we were still in the range of $70,000. I told her that she had no right to talk to me like that and hung up.*

I have not spoken to her since.

This sentence gets its own line, finishing the statement of FACTS. Missing from FACTS is any conclusion, summary, or reflection, which makes it a true chronicle, a true chronology of past events—in some ways, the only faultless history. No story, all data.

After she learned this fact, she stopped consenting to any expenses, demanded all bills of lien, an accounting of work done, dates of completion. It may seem like a simple chronology, but the logic behind this arrangement of FACTS is the belief that a woman's knowledge of information is also her consent—that, in knowing that the estimate of the cost of the house had increased each month, she was consenting to it. *She lied. She LIED* is the refrain in an interview between Goldsmith and a kind historian trying to press the matter. *She approved the house every step of the way.*

In this interview, an elderly Myron Goldsmith admits, *I thought I knew quite a bit about construction, but I probably didn't know as much as I thought I knew. I used a very bad detail at the end of the roof.*
Oh, says the interviewer.
The interviewer quickly changes the subject to floods—things outside of man's control.

———

Many documents are organized around this theory that by knowing that the house was expensive (its price shifting by the month), experimental, and potentially flawed, she consented to it. With gloved hands, I hold the three small, square photographs of her standing at Myron Goldsmith's desk. There is no way to tell what, exactly, they are looking at, but these photographs are described in FACTS as "evidence" of her understanding of the house, of her consent to its cost. These photographs are used as irrefutable proof that *she knew* the house would be unusual, knew it would have its flaws, including an unknowable budget. *She knew* becomes yet another refrain in a different interview with Goldsmith and the other young men who worked in the architect's office.
In the third photograph, though, something changes—she looks up, aware that she's being watched. In this one, she does not smile but stares through the eye of the camera in a way that pierces me.

FIGURE 12. Edith Farnsworth and Myron Goldsmith in the Mies van der Rohe office, Chicago.

It is near Christmas, and there's nobody with whom I can share any of this. I am the only person working in this archive besides one PhD student who gave birth last year. She has three hours a day to furiously work on her dissertation. She sits at the adjacent table, her fingers flying over her keyboard. I think about how we're both in our thirties—young, but women are not allowed to age. My gynecologist has already told me I am *geriatric*. I think about how far we get in our youth on the magical quality of potential and realize that in a few years, I will no longer be operating at *potential* but at *actualized* and I know instinctively, automatically how unattractive that will make me, how threatening a woman is when she is whole.

I practice this invisibility by letting things go. When I take breaks, I go to the employee kitchen. There is a machine that makes coffee for a quarter, and one afternoon, the remains of several cakes from a holiday party are scattered across a table here. I sit down and sample a few of them while staff members enter and exit without noticing me. Outside, it snows, bleak and bright.

While I think I am practicing running away, self-obliterating, I am found. The son of a colleague is working in a special research position at the CCA. I had successfully been avoiding him like I have been avoiding most people, by sticking to the edges, but he sends me an email letting me know he's having a Christmas party. And while I think I am enjoying the running away fantasy, I decide to go to the party.

There are no lights on in the entire apartment; instead, there are candles in each room. His roommate speaks fluent Russian and French with the other guests; from time to time, she breaks into English to address me. I excuse myself to the bathroom. On the way, I can see that in each of their bedrooms, they have only bare mattresses on the floor and suitcases; in hers, she has a rack of gym clothes, no closet, and no other garments. I envy the lightness with which they live.

When I join them again in the dining room, my colleague's son is speaking. He is gentle and thoughtful; he is trying to convince the administration at the CCA to fund his igloo project.

The hostess passes out on her bare mattress after making everyone gin flips, and I hold mine until it becomes warm, suspicious of the raw egg floating at the top of my glass. My colleague's son and the CCA's head curator get into an argument about whether architecture is a formal or a cultural project. I want to say it is a cultural project but not the culture of humans—the culture of capitalism, extraction, a symbol of hoarding wealth, a way of arranging that wealth and allowing others to admire it from a distance.

It's easy to trace: the way an Ivy League–trained architect whom I meet at a conference spoke slowly to me when she learned I was teaching at a state university, as if she believed that my brain might operate slower, lag behind hers, as if my brain were as shattered as the screen on my iPhone, several generations older than hers. On social media, she posts photographs of her children at a country club. They look the same as other children.

———

On my last full day in Montréal, the woman feeding me files surprises me by having no more files to feed me. I listen to her explain this in the reading room and stare at the empty table. She tells me that it's Saturday and suggests that I take a bus to the top of the mountain at the center of the city. I go back to the locker room and retrieve the boots I had just removed. They are ringed with layers of mud and ice that have begun melting away into a crust of salty sediment at the bottom of the locker.

There is a man on the other side of the locker room. He hovers in the periphery of my right eye. He does something slow at his locker as well. Placing my shoes back on my feet in silence, I feel the wet, cold street through the leather. I am enacting the reverse of my father's morning ritual of polishing his leather work shoes until they glowed, until they were nearly skin. The way he would clench his toes, a learned behavior as one of eleven children, the one who simply withdrew to be less crushed. How he would slide the foot with its clenched toes into the black sock with the gold toe and then shoe each foot. There was no other place the shoes went; they only went to work.

The shame of wearing these slippers to work in this archive makes them burn in my hands. But what is the point of shame if we do not put it into action by doing another shameful thing? I fold the blue slippers in half and slide them into my purse.

I carry these slippers with me up the mountain at the center of the city. I have no sense of direction except up and down; I get off the bus arbitrarily, at what seems like the highest point. The sky is perfect, the blue of all perfect days, and the trees wear a crystalline layer of ice, every branch gleaming as if coated in glass.

It is the same glass-looking world that the architect and his friends imagined in a chain of letters passed between them from November 1919 to December 1920 in Germany. They called themselves *Die gläserne Kette*, or the Crystal Chain. Inspired by the German revolution of the year before, the small group was sworn to secrecy, each member writing under a pseudonym. The initiator of this project, Bruno Taut, called himself *Glas* and saw a connection between God and glass, something he expressed in his infatuation with glass as a building material. *Play with fire!* he urged his companions.

His secret letters to them were full of drawings of mountains covered in glass architecture, their forms flowing over the words of each letter, crystal-line formations that were all geometry, and no humans. Underneath his drawing of a dish-like form hovering above encircling mountains, he wrote *Our world is light* and enclosed it all within the orbit of a ringed planet.

I walk down the mountain wearing the clothes I've worn every day in the archive and my one puffy coat, carrying my laptop in my purse, feeling the freeze of this new world on my face. The bus lumbers past me, leaving me alone here.

The man who inspired this chain of letters, Paul Scheerbart, was not a builder, and he was dead by the time they were written. His life's work was a prolific body of essays and novels. Among the hundreds of writings he left behind are a sea novel, a moon novel, an asteroid novel, and a glass flower novella. He seemed to *never forget that the Earth is a heavenly body*, wrote Walter Benjamin.

Scheerbart understood that architecture was an extension of culture and therefore an extension of political power. In writing about architecture, he argued that it was *too closed*, that humans need a glass architecture *which lets in the light of the sun, the moon, and the stars, not merely through a few windows, but through every possible wall, which will be made entirely of coloured glass.*

He imagined cities of glass architecture. Every new invention, he argued, brought with it a new culture. Two months after he witnessed the first flight of an airplane in Germany—when the Wright brothers appeared at Tempelhof Airport in Berlin in September 1909—he wrote an essay predicting aerial militarism and *all the kinds of death* that might come from the sky, new deaths made possible by planes, missiles, and drones. He died on October 15, 1915, starving himself in protest of this. His friends encircled him in their drawings and letters imagining utopian glass worlds in the mountains, where war would be a distant memory.

I encircle the mountain, my ears numbing first, then my nose. The white of the snow is so blinding that I can feel it in my lungs, a bright burn, as if I'm inhaling the sun itself.

In Scheerbart's asteroid novel, the sun speaks to the main character. *Terrible things always lead us forward*, it says. *Terrible things transform us.*

The sun is speaking of itself.

16.

Ancestral knowledge tells me to throw my body into the machine, let it take what it will. At times, this union feels inevitable: sitting on the side of a little twenty-foot clipper with a glass of wine as I sail down the Willamette River on a summer night, a man I barely know allowing the boat to tip so far that it threatens to spill us into the fast-moving water. I am not alone in this moment; I am part of gravity, no different than any other thing in the boat that might spill out and be carried along by the pulsing

FIGURE 13. *SCHNEE/GLETSCHER/GLAS (SNOW/GLACIER/GLASS)*.

river. I do not reach back to hold on to any part of the boat. I have no life jacket. I feel the slack of my body preparing to accept the fall. And just as the boat seems ready to capsize, it stops. We hover. And although I do not fight the possibility of falling into the churning river, I am relieved when the boat slams back into the surface of the water. The pulse of the river is not my pulse.

———

Every spring, the river rises and surrounds the house, mirroring what is above its surface while it obliterates what is below. There is no question that the river will eventually rise and erase it. When the architect built this house, he built it with the certainty of what would eventually destroy it.

Is this why he could not let go of the house? Could not untether himself from it, continued to occupy it in his own ways, even after she took ownership of it? She's excised this history out of her own archive, the letter in which she demands a rupture, a stop to this flow of money and time toward the house. The letter she writes to him on March 1, 1951, begins, *The serious confusion into which the Fox River Project has projected me serves to convince me that it is unsafe for me to close the account without the advice of a specialist competent to protect my interests.* She announces that she's turning the matter over to an attorney, Randolph Bohrer, and demands that the architect hand over waivers of lien for all unpaid bills and an affidavit giving details and dates of the work, labor, and materials furnished for the project.

Even though she has fired him, the architect designs her free-standing closet, spending his evenings in the apartment of the young man whom she had hired independently to design it, showing him how it should look, what it should be made of.

Does this in some way explain the strange letter she receives in early August in which she is informed that architectural photographers will be arriving to document the house soon for its first review in an architectural magazine? The letter is from Douglas Haskell, the editor of *Architectural Forum*, written to her and to the photographer the architect always hired, William Hedrich. The architect is sent a carbon copy. This letter isn't a request for access to her house. They already have it somehow, are coming with cameras, and presumably have keys. *We realize that undergoing architectural photography can be as heroic as undergoing a major operation. We just hope this won't faze you.* Again, with the bodily metaphors. The men inviting themselves to be surgeons, introducing themselves as such in a letter to the doctor. The initials of the editor's secretary hover at the bottom of the letter in lowercase, below the flourish of his signature.

But the house comes to life as she occupies it despite these troubles. It does so in the presence of Michael Jaffe, a man she hardly knows, a man who came to visit during a time she does not specify by month or year. He is curious about this already infamous house.

As they approach the house together, the glass door reflects both of their ghostly figures so that they can see themselves as two people on the other side of the glass, struggling to get out of the house.

When she unlocks the door, he follows her in and puts himself to work shuffling the dry wood on the travertine marble that serves as a hearth— mostly brushwood, he thinks, which will burn too fast. He lights a fire with the matches he finds scattered on the floor.

They sit on two chairs next to the small, fast-burning fire he has managed to make. It warms only their legs, and it feels like it might be burning her knees, but she doesn't move. They keep their coats on. There is nothing in the house but their bodies, the chairs they sit in, and the fire that will soon burn out. She keeps her back to the view that she knows extends behind her and never ends. If she were to turn around, to look at the plate glass wall that renders the world beyond it as a living painting, she would not know what to say. She would lose all words.

———

Such expansiveness may be accompanied by the premonition of being obliterated. It is something I avoid thinking about, though I do continue to seek out possible endings. In her memoirs, in that moment as a young woman when she feels she is *released from dimensions I was used to thinking of as my own*, it is not just the *celestial blue of the summer ocean* that catches her eye but an image of destruction: *from the veiled distance emerged Vesuvius.*

She recognizes the volcano with *a sudden throb of release.*

Ah, beautiful, seductive, sterminator Vesevo.

She underlines this for emphasis in her writing.

Vesuvius, the great exterminator.

———

It doesn't seem possible, she says to the bailiff who serves her with the court summons. (Did she see him walk up to the house? Did he knock on the glass door? Was she dressed? Did her poodle bark as he approached?)

It certainly is a pity. As long as I'm here, Doctor, do you mind if I have a look around? I've heard so much about this house—it sure is unusual.

And here, I must rely on her ability to construct a character, her own sense of dialogue and timing when she reinvents this bailiff for her memoirs. I suspend judgment and I accept her constructions. What has she turned me into, then, that I do not question her?

―――――

The *Architectural Forum* article is published in October. She has just moved in, and yet she is already imagined as being gone. The house is not meant to be a house, the reviewer argues, but *the shell within which each occupant produces his or her own dwelling.* The author implores the reader not to focus on the present but to take *the long view,* the historical view: this woman is only a *temporary tenant* of the house.

The photographs that accompany this review are the ones that she did not consent to, and they seem to be from a future in which women do not exist. In the first photograph, someone has left the glass door open—perhaps a woman has just left, or perhaps the door has always been open and

FIGURE 14. Entry and interior of Farnsworth House.

the woman has never arrived. A few chairs sit to the right of the door, side by side, facing nothing but an empty room. Her bed is cropped out of the photograph. The review goes so far as to suggest that, in fact, the human body is not the primary concern of this architecture: *The intense and special appeal of this glass prism even for those who do not at first understand it . . . is addressed directly to the spirit.*

The architect had been fired before by a client—Herbert Gericke, professor and director of the American Academy of Rome—who held a competition for the design of his house but decided against working with Mies. *I did not want to engage in a spiritual fistfight with that person over the form of a door latch.*

———

One of her poems rattles on the wall of my apartment, one I'd erased large parts of.

The wind has left you a clear echo
  : a quivering
  and thin line
of   sun.

I exist in an open, fragile state. I fulfill a series of obligations I had listed in my CV as *forthcoming*, a series of promises that must be kept in exchange for tenure. The first is a lecture in Chicago on the history of Edith and her glass house.

The problem with lecturing on her is that I have not resolved anything: I do not know whether she and the architect were lovers, I do not know with whom she had romantic relationships, am no closer to classifying her into any category, I do not know anything that cleaves the bifurcating line of truth or fiction. Instead, I stand at the podium of a lecture hall that looks out onto a busy street corner of Chicago, in a tower down the street from a series of towers the architect designed. I show images, an interpretation of this history as it has occurred through my body: an image of my body lying on the filthy ground of a borrowed garage, the light of a university projector cast over me and over a thin piece of fabric, the image of the glass house barely visible on the wrinkled cotton—*see, history is a thin, wrinkly cloth.* Images of our glass vessels, tumorous and transparent forms organized against cuttings from cold steel beams—*see, glass is a body,* I want to say; *glass is immortal, does not stop changing.* I show images of the walls of my apartment, blown out with her poems. I am

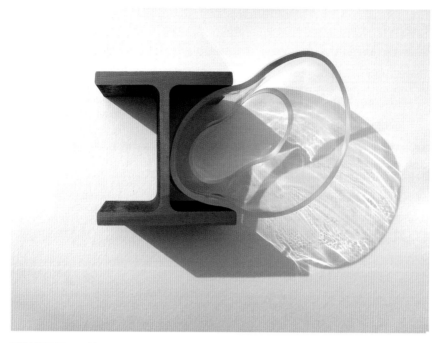

FIGURE 15. *Model No. 4.*

talking and talking, the talking becomes a line of words, some of which form sentences, and those sentences never end but gather, collectively, a web of meaning, and this goes on until I am finished, and then there is a silence, the sun setting through the glass wall behind me and over all of us, blaring into the room, and I say, *done*, and the man who had invited me says, *okay, okay*, and stands up and claps and the audience follows, uncertain, a spotty applause like rain starting to fall on concrete, and the lights turn on and the first question is from the school's historian and he says, *I am not sure whether I am glad I came to this or not*, and breathless and not listening because my own talk is thundering in my ears, I say, *Thank you.*

The next day, when I have a chance to ask the same historian what he is working on, he tells me that he is drawing labyrinths.

How do you know when it's a good labyrinth? I ask.

They're only good when I'm in love, he responds.

His students are making eggs out of papier-mâché because they are designing a bird pavilion that doubles as a space for casual sex—or maybe

I heard that wrong. I pocket one of the eggs on my way out the door, feel for its smooth secret in my hand all day as I am dragged from room to room in the school, shown their contents, equipment, and students. Once I have seen all of the rooms and all of their contents, I am escorted out.

———

When the architect was in love, he expressed it in strange ways. *God must love looking down on you*, he said to Lora Marx, his longtime girlfriend. She was taller than him.

She suspected that there was something going on between the architect and Edith, and she told this to his biographer, after his death. She had been the one to propose a break in their relationship because she thought without him around, she might have a chance to get sober, concentrate on her sculpture.

He was back in a year.

About her drinking: I don't know any more.

———

After the lecture, I receive follow-up questions in a series of emails: *How did she die?* I don't know how to answer. *What did she die of?* I have never thought of it. *Where is she buried?* This one I Google, and I reply to that email with the search link.

There is an interior to this research that touches nobody but me, a kind of being in love with this woman that doesn't require knowing much about her, if anything at all, except the things she scratched in her notebooks. All of the things she scratched in her notebooks are fragmented, which I can't help but edit and reorder myself.

I draw my eraser across lines of a Xerox until I've distilled a translated poem of hers into something I love.

And I open my eyes
and all the walls have turned to air.

The lines that I erased from this poem would not satisfy anybody's questions but my own. When I answer *I don't know*, the response to this admission is usually cross. Women are expected to answer the call of someone else's desire (for sex or knowledge). But to always be answering is a state of distraction that interferes with the *message from the beyond*, as the architect would call it, sure that the silence of his glass house was more real than the silence of me closing my eyes.

17.

I email the elderly Chicago architect to thank him for letting me sit in his living room to review the trial transcript. I request a digital copy of it, and I wait. It does not belong to him, but he has it, in the way that opportunism often insinuates itself as ownership. It had been discovered rotting in the basement of the law firm that defended the architect—Sonnenschein, Berkson, Lautmann, Levinson, and Morse—and somehow made its way into his hands.

While I wait, I look for its duplicate, its twin. The agent I reach at the Kendall County Courthouse explains that since this court case preceded digital recordkeeping, the copy they may have had—and she's not sure that they ever did—would likely have been lost when the original courthouse flooded. She explains gently that she's not going to bother to look.

———

The elderly architect with the trial transcript writes back. He has cc'ed the architect's grandson, another elderly architect. He wants to make sure that the grandson understands that I am asking for access to the transcript for *a book she is writing*, and he requests a synopsis of the book.

I tell them I do not have a synopsis yet, so they simply ask in so many words if I agree that the architect, who sued her, was the victim in this trial. *Sure*, I write back. They tell me that they will work on a contract for me to sign. They say that I must agree to never share the transcript of this trial with anyone else in person or post it to the internet. They ask for my attorney's information. *I don't have an attorney; I'm just a professor.* They ask for a superior. *My department chair?* They seem to be trying to find someone who might be in charge of my behavior, who can hold me accountable and punish me.

———

While I wait for access to the transcript, I spend time looking at the notes I'd taken on the day I was able to sit in the glass tower with all of the pages of it.

When her lawyer approaches the architect on the stand, he asks:

Q: *Were you very good friends? Close friends?*

And the architect answers:

A: *Yes, we were.*

Here is how Edith explains it:

A: *If you really want this to be clear may I explain the nature of the relationship—this was supposed to be a work of art; I was not supposed to know anything about it—I was supposed to keep out of art and stay in* ~~medicine where I belonged, and I was not shown plans [of the house]. You~~ ~~can strike that off if you want to, but that is the way it was.~~

I draw lines over the rest of her explanation. Was it the relationship that was supposed to be a work of art or the house?

People do this all the time, I tell myself, enter into a relationship of one kind or another not because they desire the other person but because they are answering the call of someone else's desire—letting the tide wash them out to sea. Or answering their own desire for something on the other side of that relationship—another way of being.

———

I try it myself. I meet a man at a conference and travel to his coast. One person slips into the space once held by another—it is common, and I am not sure how to name it.

I lose him in a museum, in a dark room full of projections of human bodies. Teiji Furuhashi's *Lovers* is presented here for the first time since Furuhashi's death in 1995. A projected image of a male body enters from nowhere and stands in front of a projected image of a woman's body, just for a moment, before turning and running into the abyss of darkness from which he had arrived. I stand in the center of the dark room, next to a tower of equipment from which the bodies are projected. It makes a throbbing, robotic beep and hum.

Is the viewer a voyeur? Are they someone who is looking? Or are they a lover also? asked a curator who interviewed the artist after he made the piece. Furuhashi doesn't understand. The curator tries again. *What kind of lovers . . . are you . . . ?* she asks, breaking her own language to try to ask him this question. It's not clear to me what she wants to know.

Lovers can be many things, he answers.

The curator is still unsatisfied. *But the lovers are quite alone. Even when they're together they're quite alone.*

Yes, says the artist, *that is my impression. They see through one another.*

She tries another way: *Is it important that the viewer knows that one of these is you? Or no? I mean, it's not a self-portrait.*

I don't know, he responds. *If I put myself in an image, I become more of myself.*

———

It is a luxury, this loneliness, this aloneness I wear like an expensive garment when I am with him. We go to cities in which loneliness feels expensive, is expensive, cities where people are knitted together out of financial necessity, like two stones in a pocket whose rough edges grate on each other.

When we are not traveling together, we send each other images of our bodies. In mine, I'm revealed in fragments. In his, he is usually enveloped in the protective fog of the mirror after a shower, his patches of dark hair further obliterating the details of his body.

One night, out of fear, I delete all the images of my body from my phone, touching the trash can icon over and over and over. But there is no erasure in the digital world—the file is just hidden until it is eventually overwritten by other data. And beyond the phone is the cloud, a link I keep breaking that mysteriously self-heals, reconnecting, reuploading all of my files so that they migrate to my laptop without my knowledge, a leaking world of images of myself. In the best ones, my face is missing, my body a series of shapes that I have never seen myself, that I can only see from my camera phone's eye, the gaze of a lover that I have imagined for myself.

18.

In the end, I receive an email from the elderly architect with permission to hire a company to go to his glass tower apartment to retrieve the transcript and scan every page without a contract in place. He gives me one vague warning—*conduct yourself professionally*—and an even vaguer threat—*guard everything appropriately and all will be well.*

One week later, the digital copies of the transcript arrive—sent by post, not over the internet. In a slim envelope that I find leaning against my apartment door are two CDs, a bygone technology. I find my external CD drive in the back of a closet, covered in dust. The scanning company has assigned a number to each volume of the transcript, anonymous and sterile. I start with MISC 001. The document begins at the end of the trial, with a list: *FINDINGS OF FACTS*.

The first "facts" are about identity and reputation: that the *plaintiff is an architect duly licensed. . . . An expert witness, Paul Schweikher, an architect, testified he considered the plaintiff as the leading exponent of creative modern architecture in the world* and that the *defendant is an intelligent, well-educated person.*

The transcript glides over my screen as I effortlessly swipe my laptop's touchpad. It takes several scrolls through legal language before I get to the charges the architect's legal team had levied against her and the charges that she had made, in turn, against the architect.

With no contract between the client and architect, there was no basis for litigation—no basis for the architect to sue the client for an unpaid bill or for fees that they'd never agreed to and no basis for the client to countersue the architect. Despite this, the architect argued that should he win the lawsuit he had put in motion, she would be *forever barred and foreclosed of all right of redemption* of the house. It would be his. She gives her deposition, her first appearance in court, on October 8, 1951, at 10:30 a.m. She is questioned by the architect's attorney, who is laying the foundation for the contractual agreement between the architect and the client to be understood as *partly express and partly implied.* An implied contract is what occurs when both parties mutually consent to an agreement without having a written contract; it is an agreement that can be expressed in words.

She filed a countersuit against the architect, referring to him as a *fraud,* someone incapable of delivering the house he had promised to build at the price he had originally quoted.

His defense argues that the *evidence will show . . . that Mr. van der Rohe, the plaintiff, is a world-famous architect.*

His defense argues that *she wanted it architecturally the way Mr. van der Rohe wanted it.*

I am learning that a woman's body and desires belong nowhere but in the male imagination. And that the institutional imagination of a woman's body is no better.

———

The same week that I am scrolling through the trial transcript, I learn that I am being accused of sexual harassment. Specifically, I learn that a student I barely know believes that we were in a relationship that soured and that I allegedly retaliated against him by giving him an undeserved low grade.

The woman telling me this introduces herself as the investigator.

I learn that when pressed by the investigator to describe the nature of our relationship, the student declared that it was limited to making eye contact in the classroom. He declared that he could infer from the fact that I made eye contact with him and from the dresses I wore that I was indeed in a relationship with him.

The investigation exists to discover whether it is possible for a relationship to exist only in a man's imagination and, if so, how much of the responsibility for that must be borne by the woman.

———

Six mortal weeks, Edith will write, describing the length of the cross-examinations during the trial. They begin once all of the paperwork is in place, at 10:00 a.m. on Friday, May 23, 1952. Her lawyer is Randolph Bohrer, a former patient who credits her with saving his life, and who is committed to defending her in court.

———

On my third trip to the Office of Equity and Compliance, I am assured that it will take a mere six weeks for the report to be completed. *Should I get a lawyer?* I ask, realizing that I have no representation in any of these meetings, nobody else to witness the questions about my body, my wardrobe, my behavior, all of which is being noted in the investigator's laptop.
   Oh, this isn't a legal process exactly, the investigator tells me.

———

Since they are suing each other, they are both plaintiff and defendant. They both serve as witness to the other's case. The trial is not made public. There is no jury. As this trial is unfolding, it is still common practice to prevent women from serving on juries in the United States. The outcome of the trial will be decided by a master in chancery instead of a jury, a local judge with some trial experience who will hear all sides of the case and write what's known as a master's report that he will submit to the presiding judge, who will make the official ruling.
   The choice to appoint a master in chancery occurs in the United States in only exceptional cases. In England and Wales, the Court of Chancery had jurisdiction over matters of equity, including the estates of lunatics and guardianship of infants.
   In the 1950s, a single woman's property fit perfectly into these categories.

———

Written on a page of her journal, a line by itself: *I suppose that ^here the contemporary notion of "credibility" would replace the older concept of truthfulness.*

———

One more thing, are you in a relationship? the investigator asks.
I think about the man who sends me images of himself, and I say yes.
She nods and types, approving of an answer for the first time.
I am never asked back for questioning after this.

———

What makes a woman believable? Not her word but the occupation of her body perhaps. The knowledge that it belongs somewhere, with someone, that it is tethered. To be made an honest woman is to be married.

Edith was also aware that the air turned around her differently than if she were a man, that even legal proceedings were a matter of narrative, that another's opinion of her—anyone's—was likely to become the truth.

She was questioned in the summer of 1952 about many things, one of which was whether she had ever heard of the architect when she first dreamed up building the house. She was accused of wanting to build a world-famous house to become famous herself.

———

I cover my body. I stop wearing lipstick. I do not take student requests for a conversation after class. I do not go to campus unless I must teach, and when I do, I take a different train or path home each day. If I do not teach, I am at home looking for other jobs and drinking wine in the bathtub. I don't cry, but my hair starts to fall out again. When the body encounters stress on top of chronic stress, it begins the process of marshaling and prioritizing resources—it performs strategic deaths.

———

There were ways in which she was tethered to him, as his doctor, mainly through his fear. He thought almost constantly about death, and she had nothing comforting to tell him; she simply answered his calls. As his physician, there was no boundary between them, and this emotional support was not a service for which she was paid. As if a woman is boundless energy, and a man is value.

He trembled even when they discussed the fireplace for the house and how he would design it. He hated what he called *black holes*. He offered her a place on the floor to set a burning log and a chimney that would carry the smoke skyward but not a fireplace. *No black holes*.

Did she ever put her hand on his knee to stop the trembling, to assure him that he was here, that he was not on the verge of falling out? In every photograph I have seen of them together, the space between them feels vast. She is often looking down, lighting a cigarette. He often stares directly into the camera, his gaze bewildered and confused.

When asked about the nature of his relationship with his client, the architect never acknowledges her assuring him that he is not dying. When pressed in deposition on the sorts of things they discussed related to the house, he says, *We talked for years about God and the world.* The cross-examining attorney dismisses him.

19.

Houses do not stand up well in a court of law, nor do the people who design them or the people who desire them.

There are days of the trial that are absolute nonsense. For an entire afternoon, she is asked whether she remembers the cost of each element of the building. The cross-examining attorney lists them as he speaks, how much the travertine had cost for the floors, and what the cost would have been if the architect had specified, instead, dry concrete. *I don't remember those specific figures,* she responds. As the attorney keeps pressing, she finally says, *I don't remember conversations with the moon—I don't remember conversations as to those specific figures.*

I don't remember conversations with the moon.

———

The inscrutable moment of truth every time she returns to the witness stand after a recess.

> Q: *Dr. Farnsworth, are you the same Dr. Farnsworth that was testifying this morning?*
> A: *Yes, sir.*

And yet, how can we be sure we are always the same—cells dying, hair falling out, a sudden memory, a racing mind or mild indigestion. Who is the same person in the afternoon as they were in the morning?

And later, when she introduces to the court the black-and-white photographs that she took of a hole in the roof—a gap between the roofing membrane and structure that allowed water to fill the glass house—they're dismissed by the architect's attorney as *trick photographs.* She has included a ruler in each photograph to measure the width of the hole precisely. How these photographs are playing a trick is never fully explained. When she describes the saturated curtains and the water dripping from the ceiling, and the water mark on the wood paneled interior wall, the architect's attorney moves to strike these descriptions as *irrelevant,* since they occurred after the date that the lawsuit was filed.

The house continues to exist, and the lawsuit would like to fix it in a time prior to its failures. The lawsuit would like to be timeless, infallible.

When she is cross-examined by the architect's attorney again, he doubts her ability to understand what she sees in front of her.

Q: You understand the word "see," do you not?
A: See, s-e-e?
Q: Yes.
A: Yes.
Q: Do you have difficulty with the word "look," l-o-o-k?

And in a poem of hers still fluttering on my wall:

Eyes rimmed with salt or rimmed with light
Give and take;
Eyes and the pain of sight,
Eyes for eyes' sake.

———

I am called back for a meeting in which I am handed the investigative report. The investigator reaches out to try to pat my hand, and I recoil. Her hand rests on the table between us.
Everything is over now, she says.
But nothing ends. Nothing will ever end.
In my office, I practice sliding my lightweight desk in front of the door, just in case. I request a classroom on the second floor, one with operable windows, from which I think I could safely jump if necessary.

———

At the end of six weeks of questioning, the master in chancery must file his report with the presiding judge, who may or may not accept his findings. It takes him a year to write it. It's been rumored that both sides, the architect and the client, made inappropriate attempts to reach out to him, to sway his report. He files it on May 7, 1953, siding with the architect. He writes that *it was proved by the manifest weight of the evidence that both parties expected the defendant to pay the plaintiff the reasonable value of his services.* Rather than the architect being required to provide a contract that clarified the financial and temporal terms of his services for his client, the master found that she, the defendant, the client, *was required to prove any claimed express or implied agreement that she was not to pay the reasonable value of said services.*

When I say the phrase *manifest weight of the evidence*, the heaviness of it almost closes my eyes. "Weight" describes the *hard burden of persuasion*, I learn from a legal website, as if persuasion were a force, like gravity, buckling our knees.

I went to receive the printed version of the transcript. I wanted to experience it physically after so much scrolling. The printer met me at the door with a dolly and helped me hoist the box into my trunk.

———

I have been accused and then exonerated of the charges of sexual harassment. I live in the accused instrument of said harassment; it is my own body—that is, someone else's interpretation of my body. I am made to sign forms indicating that I am allowing this report to be filed, under threat of losing my job. A man's imagination of my body and what it is capable of and what it desires is legitimized, alongside my appalled responses, which are recorded thus: *She strongly denied.*

I suddenly understand why, as I progressed through my undergraduate and graduate studies, the women professors disappeared, one by one, with no ceremony and no trace. They were replaced by white men, in gray or khaki or black pants, in gray or white or black shirts, with round or rectangular eyeglass frames of plastic or wire. They stood too close in the elevator, or mistook me for their teaching assistant, or invited me on dates, or suggested I was doing the wrong reading, or explicitly stated I was doing everything wrong in class.

To be told my body was wrong in the classroom was to be told these bodies, which saw my body as an object, were the correct bodies, and once again, mine was the wrong one.

———

In response to the first published review of her house in *Architectural Forum*, architects write letters to the editor. Instead of focusing on the house, they focus on her body:

I spent a lot of time figuring out the ideal female tenant of that H-beam and glass canoe and finally, with an assist from a printer in the composing room of the Oklahoma Times, *I got it. . . . "The bride is bolted together in sections and moved forward on rollers."*

The master's report argues that she must pay the architect over $30,000 or relinquish the house. The report is given to the judge, who must record an official decision. He is in no hurry to do so.

She waits, part invisible, part monster. But once she entered into the project of the house, she committed herself to being a spectacle: she found nose prints on the glass, flowers crushed by the weight of unknown bodies standing around the house's perimeter, peering in. The flutter of a skirt from behind a tree. She calls this her *invaded solitude*.

They had come to see the house, but as the house was glass, they saw her.

Her brother, Richard, dies in January 1954, months into this wait and the same year that a flood fills the interior of the house, destroying everything. She does not write about his death. Instead, she writes, *I opened the door to the house and walked around, water up to my ankles.*

A year later, in January 1955, her mother dies. The previous year's flood had destroyed the white curtains she purchased for her daughter as a house-warming gift. Edith does not write about her mother's death either but mourns *the hundreds of yards of shantung* that were lost.

After the flood, she allows plants to grow up the columns, to let the overgrowth conceal the house from the road and the river. When she had visitors, they slept on a stack of mattresses on the other side of the house from her own bed.

Glass has no history, writes Walter Benjamin, who notes that the slick surface doesn't allow for time to collect on it. *No history.* No history, no clock. She slips in and out of the house, out of time.

20.

I open a browser window and search for jobs.

I package myself for the desert. I package myself for a snowy place. I package myself for the very school that I attended, where I learned architecture. Interviews begin online first, in a video setting that connects me to New Mexico.

They want to know why I want to move to New Mexico. I am exhausted. *I really want space*, I say. There is so much truth in our ambiguities. *I want space*, I repeat into the camera attached to my computer, pinched between two desks in a kitchenette that I spent hours staging to look like a studio. *I want space.* Fronds from the two-story palm tree in the courtyard tickle my left wrist, the rest of the tree's leafy top smashed against the window glass. I push the fronds back out the window, slide the glass down.

One of the men on the search committee smiles and nods, the other two men frown and scribble things, and the staff member says *thank you* and closes the virtual window, leaving me to face my own reflection with no warning.

———

"Dinner in Yesterday's Bedroom—It's Possible with This Flexible Plan (Rooms Shifted at Will inside Glass Walls)," an article that ran in the *Chicago Tribune* in the midst of the legal proceedings promoted a house that was almost exactly the glass house that the architect defended in court. It is advertised here for the very price that he had originally promised her (half of what she paid in the end).

The reporter described the floor plan as *a remarkable new house where you can eat dinner in what was a bedroom yesterday and may be part of the living room tomorrow.* It had no operable windows, its walls were fixed panes of glass, and to air it out, you'd need to open all the doors. For privacy, curtains were provided around the perimeter of the house—*more sensible*, the architect argued—and it allowed you to create a window—that is, a line of sight, a sliver of sun, anywhere.

Eat where you wish, sleep where you wish, open the curtains to whatever you wish.

The house, despite the prominent feature in the *Tribune*, was never built. Buildings remain fixed, telling us where to sleep, where to eat, where to look instead.

The *fixed*-ness of buildings is never comfortable. A confrontation with a building can be a series of forced interactions, accidents, and violations.

———

Who was she when she occupied the house alone on long weekends, and how did the house make that version of her possible? Had she desired the house or the version of herself that lived there?

I have not yet arrived to this: I am still creating versions of myself that others can imagine absorbing. The transformation, the packaging of self for an interview is a shift from *I* (the self) to *you* (the subject) that is both disassociation and survival. The reflected image of my body as I pass a window becomes the real self: *there you are; we were looking for you.*

It is pissing on your shoes during your on-campus interview in the desert. You piss on your shoes because the toilets are too low, causing you to fall onto the seat, too far forward, and the restroom is dark, so you don't notice what you've done to yourself until your feet are wet. It's leaving the restroom and walking into the auditorium, which holds two hundred students, and giving your job talk without a microphone, because it broke before you got here and nobody bothered to fix it. *You can improvise, right?* asks the department chair whom you've just met. He hands you a large coffee. You improvise, with the energy that belongs only to a woman who has just urinated on herself, because this interview has moved into the realm of performance art.

At the end of the day, you are so tired that you fall asleep on the drive back to the hotel. The committee member in charge of driving you around gently nudges you awake in the parking lot.

It is standing in front of your closet preparing for the next on-campus interview, pulling out a black dress that won't reveal you, a black suit jacket that will box you in, and a pair of black tights. Karen Kelsky, expert on how to land your particular kind of job, advises women to wear an interview suit. *The suit can be skirt or pants, it usually doesn't matter, unless you are interviewing at an exceptionally conservative institution . . . in which case you need to wear a skirt. You should wear a sober, low-maintenance blouse or top or sweater underneath the jacket, and jewelry that is not showy or loud.*

You are walking around, breaking her rules. *I recommend suits that are not black, because black is severe. I prefer greys, browns, tweeds, etc. Black is not out of the question, however; just make sure you break it up with the top underneath and the tights.*

You are severe.

Make sure bra straps are completely hidden. Make sure your slip doesn't show beneath your skirt.

In addition to the black dress and black jacket, you throw on a pair of red suede heels and large gold earrings, explicitly against her advice not to be *showy or loud.*

You scan her website for advice specific to men on what to wear, but she doesn't give it in the same detail, because, of course, men's bodies are everybody's problem but their own. Proving this, she identifies that men have a tendency to "dress wrong" to on-campus interviews, and she advises them to turn to their girlfriends and mothers to dress them.

It is the heartbreak of an interview at the midwestern university where you did your undergraduate and graduate work, where you are hugged by all of your former professors. They have become smaller somehow. You hug the former department chair, who was once a football player and now fits between your arms. You wonder if it's professional to hold someone like this and suddenly realize this might be the last time you hug this person. Your eyes fill with tears. It's the heartbreak of discovering that you're competing against one of your former professors for this job, a wonderful professor who has been an adjunct for twenty years, all this time trying to get into a tenure track position at this university.

The students ask if you're applying for his job and ask what will happen to him if you get it. It hurts to think you won't get the job, and it hurts to think that you will. You see him and you hug him, too.

Lecture locations change at the last moment, and almost nobody is at your lecture. You remember most clearly your favorite professor and mentor from graduate school being there, a brilliant artist who has been fighting hard for you as you navigate this process, and a few students. One young woman sits in the chair right next to you while you're being introduced and shyly whispers that she loves your shoes, your bright red suede heels, right before you stand up to give your lecture.

It's a conversation with the current chair of the department of the midwestern university late in the afternoon that loops in circles, for hours, so long that the staff go home, and the office is dark around you and you start eating the fruit out of the basket on her desk, unpeeling an orange while she talks. It's saying, *Yes, that's interesting, I was thinking . . .* and she holds up her hand because she's not done. It's your phone lighting up with several text messages from your mentor, who is a member of the search committee, because dinner began thirty minutes ago: *Where are you? Are you okay?* It's you holding up your phone and she holding up her hand again. It's her question about your work. You pause, thinking about how to answer it. She jumps to her feet, ending the meeting finally with a *whoop*, because you don't understand what she asked and you're starving at the end of a twelve-hour interview, and you sit there silently staring at her with your head cocked to one side, mouth full of orange slices.

See, I got you off your game. Don't ever let anyone get you off your game.

It's returning to the university where you are currently employed, holding the letter you are required to sign, the one indicating that the tenure committee's report on your research is correct and finding that the committee hasn't accounted for a series of articles that you wrote. The chair of the department assures you that you have *done enough* to get tenure. You point out that omitting actual work you have done—research you have produced—will make it hard for you to negotiate for a higher salary, and he says he doesn't have time to change the letter, and neither does the committee.

The word *termination* is a recent memory, still metallic in your mouth, so you shut up and sign the letter, which satisfies the chair.

———

But I want to mother you, says the chair of the department at the midwestern university. She has called to offer you the job at a lower salary than you currently make and without tenure—in fact, she wants you to spend three more years in nontenured status. You think about the oranges you ate, how small they were, trying to remember how many you peeled and popped in your mouth while she spoke. *What?*

Mother you, I want to mother you.

You decline.

21.

The apartment is a use item, the architect scolds me from the pages of *The Artless Word*, a book in which his lectures have been transcribed. Most of them are lists of statements, no punctuation, all of them pronouncements of "truth."

May one ask for what?

May one ask to what it relates?

Obviously only to physical existence.

Yes, only to physical existence. I drink with an architect friend, stretch out with him on the bare wood floor of his apartment. We stare out the open windows as the world slants, the vision of it drowning out the low-grade chaos of the street below and the low-grade gray of the sky above. When he speaks, the blur of branches and leaves outside the window rasps louder than him. He has no furniture, just empty space. It has been burned into my memory as the ideal apartment.

———

I said I want space, and space—according to architectural theorist Adrian Forty—is a property of the mind. To untangle its meaning would be to untangle some part of ourselves, some navel long since healed over.

Edith, too, had her own definitions of space. They appear in the poems she translated and wrote, which blur seamlessly together:

I envision
　　Endless space beyond, and superhuman
Silences.

I hear the wind rustling among the leaves
　and the infinite pervades
me.

(Space is dark, windless, leafless and unblooming
in the micro-universe,

perhaps you saw all this, you too.)

———

New Mexico is the first place I remember vacationing with my parents as a child. We drove there from Nebraska, stayed in a roadside motel. My mother bought me tiny turquoise earrings, we ate outside, tiles under our feet, the sun baking the plaza in front of us. I remember the sky now, the same pixel sky in the many windows in front of me as I search online. I want to return to a place where my father is healthy, where his heart doesn't trouble him, where he enjoys a margarita, the sun setting, reflecting a perfect arc of light across the top of his son's head.

———

The student who imagined we were lovers has now promised that "things are going to get ugly" in an email he wrote to my department chair. I ask if we can consider this a threat and am told not to be so sensitive.

After some searching online, I discover that there is a way to make an anonymous report about a person's well-being if they are a student: the CARE team, short for Coordination Assessment Response Education. Their website puts this question first, in large blue type: *Do you know someone who needs help?* Please help me.

Do you feel:
Uncomfortable or uneasy? Yes.
Afraid for this person? Perhaps.
Scared to approach this person? Scared they will approach me, yes.
Worried things may get worse? Certainly.

A virtual wheel spins, and the website invites me to submit one CARE report.

Once it's submitted, I get an auto-response informing me that this person is no longer an enrolled student, and the assessment has been canceled.

I move toward considering things I can control. The invisibility. I think about it every day. I think about it all day. I think about it as I move about the city, usually under an umbrella. I think about it in my glass-enclosed faculty office. In the glass-enclosed main office where I sit at the conference table within view of the hallway, from which there is only one way out: through the glass door within the long glass wall. I think about it when I attend lectures in my department's dark auditorium, a room that is all one level, with two exits at the back that open up near the street that leads to a long freeway. It has terrible lighting. The edges are perpetually dark. There are long, black velvet curtains near the two back exits.

In place of invisibility, I could try reinvention. When I woke up in the desert on the morning of my interview, I remember how arid it was, how straight my hair fell, how I was someone else. I was a woman who could hide behind her sheet of straight hair. I did just that, let it fall over my face for a frantic ten minutes at the podium while I tried to memorize everything I'd printed for my job talk, an impossible task. When I put my hand up to smooth it away from my face, I was a new person, a woman who didn't need those notes. I was a woman who could package herself over and over again as she sought more livable wages, better housing, a landscape that didn't contain the promise of earthquakes, a place not threatened by climate precarity. But then, what place is not?

When asked why I was trying to leave my current teaching position, I said I loved the desert, because I could not say, *a former student of mine might want to kill me.*

What to do with the endings that appear, that do not align with a typical chronology but tear through with abrupt force?

The accountant that the architect hired, the one who convinced him to go through with the lawsuit, dies by suicide. A page turns. *If we were quiet, we would hear ourselves as electric dust,* Edith writes. There is no context to this thought, another idea punctuating the memoirs that I could follow or not follow, to no conclusion in particular.

———

The chair at New Mexico writes to let me know that they'd be glad to hire me, that I am meant to sign and accept the salary offer immediately. It is almost $10,000 less than I currently make. I'm told it will be impossible to negotiate. It is spring break, and in a blind rage, I buy a ticket to fly to the East Coast, to suspend myself in air for as long as possible while remaining in the same country. I don't want to touch the surface of the planet anymore.

I visit the man who sends me photographs of himself. There is a strange shape to the interior of his condominium because he stole it. It's a shape I spend the entire next day studying, drinking his beer while he is teaching. There isn't language to describe this shape—it's the result of him breaking through the ceiling and stealing the building's attic, then placing smooth white drywall and plaster against the interior of the attic's roof. It is faceted, white and flawless, a sort of jagged dome that sails overhead, no matter what room you are in.

———

Strange things leak into the press while she waits to learn if she will stay in her house or be forced out. She is interviewed in *House Beautiful* twice, complaining about the house and its transparency—how it forces her to stay on alert at all times, how she cannot place a trash can without worrying about it being seen from the outside, and the incredible cost to heat the house. In the first of these two articles, she is unnamed. Author and *House Beautiful* editor Elizabeth Gordon warns readers that the European "cult of austerity" is coming for them, too: the house is a literal threat to American democracy.

In between advertisements for Lev-i-lor blinds and the Wonder Action Attic Stair, *House Beautiful* runs a "fable" about an emperor whose trickster architect builds him a cellophane castle through which the entire population watches him walk about in the nude—a spin on "The Emperor's New Clothes" that substitutes walls for the garments. *His castle is nothing at all!* cries a child. The dejected emperor sits naked on the floor of it, exposed, flesh folding over flesh. Where Edith had complained about the fear a woman can feel exposed behind glass walls—the real vulnerability of it—this fable is meant to appeal to any men in the audience, reminding them of the mortal danger they would face in the same predicament: looking like a fool.

———

Instead of quitting my job, I ask for a leave of absence for one year. It is possible that I will want to return. In being "absent," a part of me remains. I try to give up my keys. *But it's just a leave of absence*, protests my department chair. I place them in an envelope and shove them to the back of my campus mailbox. All that will remain in the empty office: two empty white desks, seven empty white shelves, one empty white file cabinet. Absence implies that you should be present, that a place has a right to expect that presence. I allow them the language but take all of my presence.

———

The judge retires without rendering a decision on the trial. A new judge assigned to the case determines that despite the lengthy transcript, without a written contract between the two parties, the architect has no right to the fees he's demanding, nor does he have a right to seize or sell the property from under her. The judge tells the two sides they must settle.

She writes a check for $2,500. By 1956, the trial is over. The architect never builds another house.

She returns to the house on the weekend. It's hers now. What is there to celebrate?

———

I open an expensive bottle of red wine and call the chair at New Mexico to accept the offer of less than I currently make. They will email me the paperwork. I open the wine and take my time drinking it, letting sunlight stream through the glass and cast red light onto the white surface of my desk, watching the red color deepen by the hour until it is gone.

I spend the last day of my lease sitting in my empty apartment. I fall in love with it again, the glow of the promise of open space. It is space after all, not objects, that I was after. Space, though, isn't innocent. Space is the many windows opening and collapsing on my laptop while I search for apartments in New Mexico, trying to determine which portion of limitless space I will rent, what I can afford. Such transactions form a biography, a whole life, my whole life.

22.

The lawsuit ends, and her memoirs are no longer chronological, no longer sentences, but begin to occur scattershot across her journals and notebooks. The external world rarely makes an appearance. In place of sentences, I find fragments of her own philosophy, poems she is translating, and poems she wrote, often with no indication of authorship, a slippage that frustrates me while it draws me further into this interior world.

> *No, I won't add more wood*
> *to the fire we'll let*
> *what's there burn down*
> *little by little*
> *and the flame turn gradually*
> *into ember*
> *and you and I seated in silence*
> *side by side—waiting from the darkness*
> *of the room as even*
> *(even) the embers finally*
> *burn ^out^*
>   *down.*

Historians have tended to approach her poetry as if it contains some confession. Tour guides at her house will sometimes include a dramatic reading from one of her poems when they bring guests into the area in which she slept.

> *I woke*
> *To hear some flying creature strike the pane*
> *Of glass beside my bed—strike and flutter*
> *For a moment, strike and beat.*

This poem seems to bear the uncomfortable weight of being evidence that she was miserable in the house, that she was crushed in some irremediable way by the process of building it, by the fact of her solitude in the structure, and—perhaps, it's not so subtly suggested—by her "loss" of the architect.

Unseen wings slipping down the pane of glass.

> *And in the grass*
> *Below, there lies*
> *My hope, and dies.*

But I have never approached her poems as confessions: I believe that they accurately reflect the slow, beautiful, and often cruel events that unfurled in the natural and humanly constructed world around her.

———

Edith wrote roughly one hundred poems and entrusted them all to an editor named Jim Gerard. In the early 1970s, she asked him to find a publisher for them: he was never successful in doing this. Ultimately, thirty years later, he gave them to the archivist at Northwestern Memorial Hospital, her former employer, along with a letter in which he expresses his relief that she will take them. *I must admit that much of it is too high brow for me,* he writes. *It is good to know that all this work has found a home.* Home in storage in an auxiliary building in an industrial part of Chicago.

When I visit the hospital archive to view this collection, the poems are stacked neatly on a desk. I photograph them one at a time. There are hundreds of them, meticulously typed on thin paper. The collection has no title; in a letter to Gerard, Edith simply refers to them as a *volume of my own poems written over the last dozen years.*

———

This collection of poems was written sometime between the late 1950s and the early 1970s, the period during which Edith took legal ownership of her house and built a life in it. Her experience of living here is best recorded in this poetry. Other parts of her life are more traceable, easier to put into a chronology: those that reference her documented conflicts or entanglements with men.

Men and the patriarchal structures that advance them are the air we breathe, the atmosphere, a resistance we experience like gravity—the thick medium through which we struggle to live or simply die but always in relation to them. And perhaps she understood the house to be a rupture in that oppressive medium—if so, we can read the poems as time and space entirely liberated from male occupation, coercion, control. The poems are about the ordinary and the horrific, the animals that are born and die in the space under the glass house, the interiority of her loneliness often, and the intensity of the natural world from which she is separated by a mere pane of glass:

> *Is it time to light the lights? The rain*
> *has passed, but now the nights*
> *fall early and the cicadas are in bloom.*
> *Tent caterpillars flower and pollinate; aphids*

consume the roses; sour are the apples
on the winter tree; slow, the flights
of swallows in the dusk. The strain
of dark and light is vast, the August
green of leaves and grass turns black.
The day is gone, and frost is at the glass.

———

I am here too late. In fact, I would not be here at all except that the archivist emailed me. I did not even know this collection existed. The man writing the book about Edith knew, somehow, and has already been here. I am sheepish, grateful, feeling a bit stupid. *He didn't spend much time with the poems*, the archivist explains, as a consolation. She brings me a cup of coffee, and we talk about the poetry, how difficult it is to parse.

A collection of poems can contain the life that one is living or has lived, perhaps a life one has never lived but felt or imagined might be possible. In this collection is a poem dedicated "To M.G.P.," initials that recall Mary G. "Polly" Porter, one of the women reclining on the rocks in the Castine photograph.

"J'accuse"
To M.G.P.

You have beaten me with whipped cream
And I am churned with butter.
This has been in winter and in June.
I mention it, enumerate to utter
What I suffer from your flagellations.
Is it too soon for me to say so or too late?

Cold have been the sunsets,
Windy the fall of night, and the driving rains
Have whipped our shabby driftwood shores;
The spruces tumbled in the hurricanes
—Would it be from cataclysm, loss or butter
That I suffer?

She does not include a date on this poem. The initials, M.G.P., serve as both a form of erasure and a signal that I could try to read but never fully interpret. And yet, as Susan Stewart writes, *poetry is a force against effacement. To make something where and when before there was nothing. J'accuse*, a phrase that is a common expression against a powerful opponent. Here, *J'accuse* arrives with a wink, the accused has beaten Edith with whipped cream, churned her with butter—either these delightful flagellations of being beaten or churned, so to speak, or the end of them is the cause of suffering. These events—real or imagined—are described as occurring in June and in winter, when Edith and Polly would conceivably have seen each other in Castine and in New York City. To read a poem that hints at the queer erotic among her collection is a relief, a signal to me of her humanity, her sense of humor, her sensuousness; to add the initials of a woman who was as good as married to someone else, a bold move to leave open to interpretation. Perhaps, compiling this collection in the early 1970s, from Italy, she felt the freedom to do so. And perhaps in this paragraph, I've done what so many historians have done before and projected a desire onto her. And yet, these are expressions of a life that I wish she'd left more evidence of, more fragments to align.

What lies slumbering in all words, Stewart writes.

In 1960, Edith would publish an essay in the *Northwestern Triquarterly* arguing that poetry's great themes have been dislocated by contemporary society—nature, in particular, has become too domesticated, she writes, and love . . . *everybody knows what has happened there. It has died from exposure. It has been raped by self-appointed psychiatrists, clubbed by opportunists, and left by boors to perish.* Psychiatrists even well after the 1970s would advance theories of *lesbian psychosis*, as Lillian Faderman writes, which became big business for post–World War II psychoanalysts, who believed (and lectured, wrote, and "treated" patients as if) lesbians were incapable of happiness, disordered. Whether this was Edith's personal experience or not, as a physician and medical researcher, she was certainly acutely aware of it.

———

"*Was it a white habit and a black horse, Polly, or a black habit and a white horse? And were you always galloping so romantically?*" The quotes around this comment signals that they are words Edith puts into someone else's mouth when she writes about M.G.P. in her memoirs. And then, in her characteristic way of fragmenting the past, a flash of her first childhood experience with jealousy—her mother advising her that *human beings commonly suffer*

from jealousy and that all she could do was to bear it and try to control it.
Jealousy of what or whom remains unclear.

When shall I pick the long-loved moon, follows a line from her poem,
"Images of Love."
And clip from the stem her satellites?

The pages that went missing from Edith's memoirs would fill in some
of this mystery. They may have been removed by well-intentioned friends.
It's possible they were torn out by Edith herself at the last minute. She
intentionally left a body of work—the memoirs, poetry, and photographs—
through which to know her. What the pages said, if indeed they ever existed,
can never be known.

Why was I so slow to recognize that the women who had first introduced
her to the architect, Georgia Lingafelt and Ruth Lee, had invited her to
this arranged dinner in their home? In Lingafelt's obituary in the *Chicago
Tribune*, Ruth is referred to as Mrs. Edward H. Lee and she is Miss Lingafelt.
This obituary explains that Miss Lingafelt and Mrs. Edward H. Lee were
friends who "made a home" together. Nothing more is said.

———

I can line up the photographs that I have found of this period; in all of
them, Edith is smiling. In my favorite one, she is lounging on the porch of
the house in what look like beautiful pajamas, having coffee with a friend,
Beth Dunlap, one of her patients. Beth's husband, Bill Dunlap—the young
architect who designed the wardrobe in the glass house and the screens
around its porch after Edith broke with the architect—is the eye behind
the camera. Her face is upturned—she smiles at Beth, her hands cradling a
white coffee cup, the poodles on the porch sniffing. This image is resonant
with the photograph of the women in Castine—she is making a home.

How to explain this? That she found space and pleasure in her life in the
glass house and, in finding this—with friends and alone—she evades cat-
egorization, collections, archiving, indexing, identifying. The same expansiveness that she found in her youth when traveling alone, she found here,
living alone. Living alone, traveling alone as a woman: the world is yours to
consume rather than the other way around—when I am alone, time cannot
put its tenterhooks into me. And although the first reviewer of the house
writes that this is precisely what the house was for—*it is addressed directly*

FIGURE 16. Edith Farnsworth and Beth Dunlap, c. 1951.

to the spirit!—even later historians cannot accept that she experienced the house in a way that she enjoyed, that the architect could make an instrument for this.

As she lives in it, the glass house becomes less transparent. She takes a series of photographs of the house. In these, the grass is so tall that it bends like waves tossed in a high wind and brushes the underbelly of the structure as if the house had finally become a ship afloat. The branches of the trees get long, heavy with leaves, and they arc over the house, sheltering it from the sun and darkening the interior so that we cannot peer in.

What I would like to tell her is that she has a right to her opacity. She has a right to be impossible to decipher. That I refuse to do the violence of finding what she has not left out for me, in the open, or the equal violence of speculating on her life.

———

I have also lived in unmarked ways. To sever my ties with Oregon, I used all of my university research funds as quickly as possible, knowing that I would never return. I rented an entire house in Dublin for a week, a place

FIGURE 17. Edith Farnsworth House.

for my mother and me to stay: her first international trip. The university-approved reason for the trip was for me to research Irish architect Eileen Gray, but the real reason I chose Dublin is that my mother's side of the family emigrated from Ireland, and she'd always wanted to visit. From the house I rented, we could walk to the city center and catch trains to any part of the country. In the evenings, I watched her write in her journal, recording visits we'd made to crumbling cathedrals, restaurants, small towns we'd reached by train, the man in boxer shorts we'd watched do a high-wire act in Galway (she covered her eyes and laughed), the trains we'd almost missed, the kid on the train selling candy who cajoled us into buying Cadbury bars and tea. I watched her while she sat alone at the center courtyard of the house under a darkening sky. I thought about all the time I'd missed spending with her because I was living hundreds of miles away; how far away I would still be after my move. That even though this move was a step toward a more stable career, I would still be making just enough money to survive. The distance, in the end, meant nothing material except that every time we see each other, we will have grown older. How what she was writing was at once a celebration of her own intellectual life and purpose and a record of how rare was our time together. When she wrote on those evenings, it was as if there was a light above her, her concentration so fierce that it almost combusted in the air.

23.

Her sensitivity toward the ineffable, that which is felt but cannot be expressed, made her an excellent physician. Her patients came to her suffering with the unseen. In her memoirs, she does not specify what ails them. *The common human day is full of signs of impatience and bad temper*, she tells the forty-year-old unmarried librarian who flicks dishcloths at her mother. *Would it be sensible of us to magnify these little outbursts into serious disorders? Call them by the old familiar names of "impulses" and "upbringings" and be glad of them.*

Edith is working to correct what the librarian has just been told by her psychiatrist: that because she did not get married at the right time, her repressed sexual drives have made her hostile, uncontrollable, and damaged. But the woman cannot say the word "sexual," so instead, she continues to repeat the phrase *my drives.*

It's my drives, Doctor.

In this, we can begin to read the coded language of post–World War II American psychoanalysts for whom *drives* were seen as those uncontrolled libidinous urges of the "repressed female homosexual."

———

By the mid-1950s, unmarried women were considered deviants. *Sexual Behavior in the Human Female*, published in 1953, found that "female homosexuality" existed primarily among single women and was, in Alfred Kinsey's words, a *psychological problem*. This report was recognized by a *Newsweek* reviewer to contain some errors *when a woman mentally distorted her first sexual experience out of all proportion to its value or was unable to understand when it took place.* There is no reflection on the fact that only a child or an adult unable to consent would not understand when a sexual experience took place. The review is accompanied by a photograph of the authors: eight white men sporting the same suit and same haircut sit around a table with piles of paper, furrowing their brows. *Kinsey and his co-workers compiling another best seller* is the caption.

A man enters her office to explain that he tends to collapse *like a dry twig that somebody a lot stronger had snapped over his knee.*

What did you do? she asks the salesman, who had an episode of what he calls *collapse* at work.

Said a prayer that came back to me empty.

Family history?

My father used to kick a dishpan down the basement steps.

To another patient, with another unspoken malady, she explains,

You have been talked into an interpretation of your life and self which has shocked and frightened you, a crude and violent interpretation which is completely unsuitable to you, but because it was offered by a person with authority you feel that you must accept and believe it.

Despite these reassuring words, she is also one of the editors of the 1955 edition of the *Passavant Memorial Hospital General Information and Rules for Guidance of the House Staff and Clerks.* In this document, she clarifies that since attempted suicide is a misdemeanor, if patients enter by way of the Emergency Room, a report should be filed with police. And *it is essential that any stomach washings or vomitus, including that obtained in the Emergency Room, be collected, labeled with the patient's name, hour, and date, and saved for the Coroner or Toxicologist, or until the attending physician has discharged the patient. Any partially digested or intact capsule will be saved as well. This is necessary to meet legal requirements.*

After discovering this passage, I spend the rest of the afternoon staring out the window, thinking about Ellen. The way my aunt had called me to the phone, how she had watched my face as my mother relayed the news to me, the bowl of potato chips she offered while I waited for my mother to come pick me up, sitting in my numb disbelief as I said goodbye to my uncle and cousins who were going to mass to pray on it.

How nobody mentioned the word, nobody would say suicide. How everyone spoke as if she was a child, not a teenager. The way the priest, at her funeral, described her as an angel looking down on us peacefully, as if she had not suffered in life and death, as if dead girls were ordinary, unexceptional, as if it was normal the way nobody asked why she looked so thin and exhausted, as if it was normal, the way she excelled at everything silently. As if it was normal, the way the popular girls in school, the ones who drew her into their circle, would tell her they hated her, then say it was a joke. As if it was normal, the way she could hold your gaze, could see you, noticing something as small as a new haircut and say, *You're a new woman today.*

As if it was normal, the way we were just girls, but the world decided we were women, the way we all tried that word on. At fifteen or sixteen my classmates were on the cover of *Bride* magazine, modeling dresses—*Child Bride*, we called it, congratulating the most recent sophomore girl who was on the cover, breasts just in, holding hands with a 40-year-old man, a model who stood in as the groom.

We were children, and then suddenly, we were accelerating toward death, could not mature fast enough for a world that knew exactly what it wanted to do with us.

Every year, around the time of her death, I look again for her obituary. I have never found it. It has been a quarter of a century.

———

In her employer's archive, I am not allowed to look at documents side by side: I am required to open one folder at a time, to progress in a linear way through the documents inside. But I would like to take the poem she writes about a young man's suicide and place it atop her *General Information and Rules for Guidance of the House Staff and Clerks* to show that she wasn't so clinical—to say that I believe that she would have been more compassionate than this, would not have allowed an attempted suicide to be charged by police. That she would have forgotten to save the *vomitus*, would have been stone-faced in the presence of authority.

But I cringe when I read it, the transactional and clear-minded way that she imagines the young man's suicide letter:

> *I want to leave my bike*
> *to the fellow who has the room across the hall.*
> *I'll need his gun.*
> *I'm sorry to make trouble*
> *for Mrs. Swansen. She'll hear the shot and fall.*

Those of us who are alive are left to imagine what meaning this life holds, left to hypothesize that even in suffering, life is better than death, while we know only half the story. And yet, when you lose someone to suicide, I can tell you that the opening it tears in the world is one that never mends. You just tend to it, gentle with the edges.

———————

Death lives longer than life, she writes.

———————

The archivist points out a surprising coincidence that appears in the hospital records but nowhere else. That her brother, Richard, died at Passavant Hospital, where Edith worked, in 1954. He was only forty-three years old. He was a salesman employed by a Chicago-area insurance company. He did not take on any role in the family lumber business, as far as I can tell, and had no children. He married a woman, and they moved into a house shortly before his death.

When I ask about him, Edith's nephew—her sister Marion's son—just says, *He wasn't a very strong man.* I know not to press. I tell him thank you. *Thank you,* he responds. Richard's obituary is equally terse: it was published a day after he died, announcing that he would be buried the following day.

———————

The archivist also shows me a report drafted by the Medical Board at Northwestern University expressing concerns about how Edith had been managing a patient under her care. I sift through the pile of correspondence to try to learn what she had done in the treatment of the patient that was found to be inappropriate, and the archivist laughs. She tells me there's no chance it can ever be found—when doctors face disciplinary action or when concerns about them come up, she says, those documents tend to disappear.

Is it that she refused to refer patients to the electroshock therapy? Is it that she would routinely admit and keep patients overnight at the hospital who were having breakdowns, writing to their employers in coded language to explain that they were unwell, were being treated in the hospital, and would return when they were recovered? Is it that she discharged her friend Jenny Geering from the hospital by simply wrapping a fur coat around her and driving her home?

Silence.

This silence becomes a leave of absence that she takes from the Northwestern University Department of Medicine. In her memoirs, there is no mention of it. She lets her office lease run out on May 1, 1967. By 1968, she is no longer teaching and suspends her practice. The department chair sends her letter after letter: is she intending to return after her leave of absence? Will she at least take the equipment that they've been storing for her? Does she approve of their decision to pool her research funds with the department general funds? She doesn't respond. And finally, the chair writes, *continuation of your leave of absence is dependent on a satisfactory request and explanation.*

What does it say that in order to stop being a doctor, she simply lets the lease run out on her office. What does it say that without the space to practice being the things we say that we are, we simply stop being them. What does it say that I'm not asking you these things—no question marks—I am telling you.

24.

I get emails from my colleagues in Oregon: *Where are you? School is starting.* I tell them I moved to New Mexico. Some write back; most do not.

Everything I own is packed into boxes that the university-mandated movers stacked up high in a back bedroom of the house I am renting from a new colleague in Albuquerque: it has bare plywood walls and a rickety staircase to a mezzanine level. I am only supposed to occupy the finished parts of the house, the rooms that her mother lived in as she died slowly over the course of the past year. I poke at the boxes at the top of the pile with the handle of the broomstick and each one splits open like a ripened fruit when it hits the floor, my old things rolling out. I repeat this until I have enough things from enough boxes, leaving the vast majority of them packed, their contents a mystery until I notice something is missing. It's better this way, living in scarcity, the back room flush with things that I long for, then forget.

Her mother's furniture is still in its place. I walk around the house, touching these things that her mother had touched. I live here because I can only afford to finish someone else's sentences, unable to pay the price to start and finish my own.

———

How did death touch Edith? In her early sixties, when she turned away from medicine, she would likely have been past menopause. I stand at the sink, washing dishes through a hot flash, my first. My insides molten, moving like lava, legs trembling, sweat on every inch of me. Death just touching his fingertips to my lower back, letting me know, getting acquainted, reminding me that he is waiting. I bend until my forehead touches the kitchen counter and I breathe until he leaves.

Did hot flashes stir her to finish the work she felt she needed to finish? I begin to write my sentences faster, jot down each spasm of thought before I lose it. Freedom, not children, was the dream in me, and now that I have it, death waits.

> *Now everything is getting to move slowly,*
> *much slower than it used to move when*
> *you were hurrying to die*, she writes in an untitled poem.

———

I open a box labeled "Kitchen." Inside of it is the one saucepot and one soup pot that I own, and inside of these, wrapped in bubble wrap, two small concrete heads I received as a gift from the artist who made them—a mother and a child. The child's head is so small I can hold it in the palm of my hand, his lips shaped perfectly, a puckered little mouth. There are metal filings on the surface of the concrete. They pierce my fingertips. I place the heads on what I have decided is my writing desk, in a room with lace curtains over the window, facing west. The room fills with light as the sun descends, sinking behind the highway—a horizon of speeding cars in front of a backdrop of dormant volcanoes.

———

The history of human inhabitation in New Mexico can be traced back at least 21,000 years. It is evident in the ancient fossilized human footprints found by researchers examining the dunes—an ancient lakeshore—at White Sands National Park, which is completely surrounded by the White Sands Missile Range, the largest active military installation in the United States. Spain arrived in New Mexico in 1540 and was expelled in 1680 by Indigenous Pueblo people, joined by the Hopi and Zuni, Apache, Ute, and Navajo to end the horrific violence they had been subjected to, overthrowing Spanish colonial settlements and destroying land ownership records. The remaining colonists fled, only to return thirteen years later, completing a "reconquest" that claimed large tracts of land for Spanish officials. By the early eighteenth century, Indigenous homelands here were deeply colonized, subjected to Spanish, and later, Mexican rule. Po'su wae geh Ôwîngeh, *drink water place* or *water gathering place*, was renamed Pojoaque Pueblo, Nąngbe'e Ôwîngeh, *born of the earth and the fertile imagination*, became Nambe Pueblo, Tets'úgéh Ôwîngeh, *village of the narrow place of the cottonwood trees*, became Tesuque Pueblo—just three of the nineteen Pueblo communities that, with three Apache tribes and the Navajo Nation, are part of the twenty-three tribes located in New Mexico.

One of my students tells me that it is increasingly difficult to maintain your tribal enrollment. The Bureau of Indian Affairs measures this by a percentage of one's blood belonging to one specific Nation—the "blood quantum" system established by the federal government. He tells me that in order to claim enrollment with the Navajo Nation, his mother's tribe, he had to file paperwork with his father's tribe asking them not to claim him as a member. If he has children, their claim to membership will be entirely based on their mother's tribal affiliation, assuming they meet the blood quantum requirement of one quarter or more. *Genocide by bureaucracy*, he says. Through this process, generation by generation, tribal membership could will "cease to exist" in the eyes of the government.

———

When the county proposes to condemn two acres of the property Edith purchased for the glass house to improve the roadway for public safety, she obsessively counts cars on the dangerous eighty-three-year-old single-lane bridge, arguing that there isn't enough traffic to merit improvements to it. When that doesn't work, she develops what the local newspaper describes as an *amateur interest in archaeology.*

By the time the county files its condemnation suit on September 1, 1967, she has determined that the land her house is on is—as she describes it—*the last remaining untouched camping site of the East-West crossing of the Indian tribes in the area.* The suit goes to trial, with three landowners pressing charges against the county for condemning their property. The examining lawyer asks her for more information on the specifics of the land:

Q: *Is this camp site recognizable? Could I go down there and see it? What does it look like?*
A: *No.*
Q: *Why not?*
A: *It is underground.*
Q: *So, in order to see it, you would have to dig it up?*
A: *That is right.*
Q: *So, as of right now, you cannot point out this particular camp site?*
A: *Yes, you can point it out as to where it is.*
Q: *You say it is underground, you cannot see it?*
A: *Well, the litter is on the surface. Yes, I can show you in the plowed fields.*

The jury never goes to the plowed fields to look at what has been violently brought to the surface, broken up into pieces and scattered where crops were planted for generations. *Indians, long since gone from the area* is how, in 1968, *Chicago Tribune* journalist Ann McFeatters described the people on whose unceded land the glass house is located.

Or *probably, and I say probably because nobody can pin these things down definitively*, begins a man named Richard Young—an expert in this trial for some reason, a man who describes his qualifications as forty hours of graduate work at Loyola University in psychology and eight hours on the study of architecture at the University of Illinois—*this is one of the major Indian camp sites in this area . . . representing all of the "primitive" cultures beginning here about 10,000 years ago when the*
[   ] *retreated up to the time when the French and Illinois Indians occupied this.*

There is a hole in the transcript, an unknown—perhaps the court reporter meant to fill it in later, or perhaps she saw the blank space and thought it wouldn't matter. The newspaper uses the term *pre-historic* but also identifies the Indigenous community as the *Hopewell*, after Mordecai Hopewell, the farmer on whose property mounds were found and excavated in the 1800s. *Hopewell* does not define a specific people but a civilization that was comprised of a network of precontact Native American cultures.

Red and yellow stakes are placed on her property, outlining the center and edges of the bridge road.

In her notebook, Edith practices translations, a fragment of a poem:

Who knows what lies below?
Too small are the holes made by my eyes
through you.

————

In the trial transcript, the evidence of Indigenous people is banished to the past, to history, in the way that whiteness displaces everyone and everything else around it.

She is desperate to keep the land, so she draws up a deed promising it to the state for (continued) *archaeological exploration* once she dies, on the condition that they do not seize any of it to build the road. She hires archaeologists who argue that the expansion of the road will ruin this "historical treasure," but she says nothing about ceding the land to existing Indigenous people. *From my hands to yours,* she whispers to the state of Illinois.

She is so sure that they will accept this offer that, during the trial, she says—on the very day that the deed is drawn up, March 1, 1968—*I am no longer the owner. I believe the Department of Commerce of the State of Illinois is now the present owner.*

Her own lawyer presses her: *That is by a deed of gift from you, that correct?*

A: *Correct.*
Q: *To preserve this as an archaeological site?*
A: *For investigation, yes.*

The state of Illinois does not acknowledge or accept the deed to the land.

––––––

While the white spatial imaginary sees water and land as properties belonging to (white) people, Nick Estes writes that for the Očhéthi Šakówiŋ, for example, the Missouri River is a nonhuman relative who is alive. The Fox River lies just one hundred feet from her house in the Fox River Valley.

According to a report on the archaeology of this site authored by Rebecca S. Graff:

> *The Indigenous groups that lived in the area around the Edith Farnsworth House site into the Euro-American contact period include the Illinois (also called the Illini or Illiniwek), Wea and Piankeshaw, Potawatomi, Ojibwe, Odawa, Mesquakie (Fox), Sauk, Ho-Chunk, and Kickapoo. These Indian Nations can be broken down into three categories: resident people, such as the Illinois, who had lived in the area for thousands of years; refugee populations from the Atlantic seaboard who fled their homeland to escape war and encroaching European settlement; and temporary allies or opponents from areas south or west of the Great Lakes. Still, the bounded separation into different "nations" is itself a product of Euro-American colonial expectations rather than the lived experience of indigenous Illinoisians.*

Beyond this, the Kkaskaskahamwa (Kaskaskia), Myaamia (Miami), Očhéthi Šakówiŋ, Peoria, and Shawandasse Tula (Shawanwaki/Shawnee) peoples also have ties to this land.

Many of these are Anglicized names. Fox, for instance, is an exonym, the name used by the American government, derived from a French mistake during a previous colonial era: the French applied the name *Fox,* an overheard clan name, to the entire tribe who spoke the same language, calling them *les Renards*. The *Mesquakie*, or *Meskwaki*, call themselves *Meshkwah-kihaki*, meaning "the Red-Earths," derived from a creation myth in which *Wisaka* created the first humans out of red clay.

But people are never mentioned in the trial transcript: just the *litter*, the *potsherds*, and other evidence of life, as if that life ceased to exist, as if the descendants are not a part of this history.

In Graff's report, the findings at archaeological sites within several miles of the Farnsworth House are described, including a mound that was bull-dozed in the 1950s to reveal twelve burials: *when surveyed, the site was found within a plowed corn field . . . the owners reported that there had been "fragments of 5–6 skeletons reportedly removed from the limestone lined pit."* Removed to where, by whom, and when is not clear.

Since value is not ascribed to the bodies of those who were displaced, the attorneys use money as their value system. But it's arbitrary: nobody can put a number to the monetary value of this land. In a desperate attempt to do this, John Maxon, the associate director of the Art Institute of Chicago, is invited as an expert witness to this trial, and he puts a specific price on the land. He bases this figure on what he guesses the glass house itself is worth: between $250,000 and $350,000. He arrives at this number because this is how much the Picasso sculpture in downtown Chicago is worth, the one down the street from Mies's Federal Center. When pressed to explain this price, he says that it is the price of a *major work of art by the man who is considered the most distinguished, indeed the greatest architect of this century.* The condemnation of two acres of land and the widening of the road, he argues, would . . . *destroy in a large part the concept . . . of this glass box set in infinite-seeming distance.*

If the road came closer, the examining lawyer asked, *could this house be sold at all, would it have any buyers?*

I am convinced that as the house stands in its present setting there is undoubt-edly a market from people who would view it with real pleasure and are prepared to pay for that pleasure, Maxon answers. It would no longer be possible, with the road and new bridge being moved closer to the house, to look *from the porch off into what to the eye seems an indeterminate distance.*

And this is the true value of the house: to allow one to stare into the middle distance, unbothered.

———

When I write about this for a short article, the editors send the draft back. In the comments, one of them poses a question to another, perhaps unaware that it is never deleted: *Is she raising this point for her own gratifica-tion? Does she have connections to the Indigenous community here?*

They're paying me $250. I ask whether they expect me to delete this part of the history of the house. I don't get a response. I'm invited to a meeting in which I'm told that under no circumstances should I reach out to local Indigenous communities. I'm to focus only on chronology; it's history I'm writing, after all.

Where do I put this, then? That minutes into her sworn witness tes-timony, Edith whines, *It is my fortune, so I am told, to be astronomically wealthy. This is a false statement.*

———

I, too, am an itinerant single white woman, waking up daily in a place that I have no claim to and in which I am not particularly helpful or needed. My skin knows this, bursting open on the surface, the dry air drawing every drop of moisture out of me so that all day I scratch at myself.

A student shows me a picture on her phone—it is the Spanish land grant that her family has had since the 1600s. My students speak to each other in Spanish before class begins. I smile and unpack my laptop at the lecture podium, have nothing to contribute here. They offer me the angli-cized versions of their names. Even when I tell a young woman that I can pronounce her name, *Angela*, the way it's intended to be said, she smiles and says, *No, that's for my family and this is school. You can say it the way my other teachers say it here.*

The faculty is predominantly white, and the students are described on the university website as predominantly Hispanic. One of my students tells me not to use that word; it's the *language of cops*, he says, and I never utter it again.

———

Estes, too, explains that the Lakota had to come up with a word that described white man's law as they continued to encounter it in the nine-teenth century. Their word was Woope Wasicu, or *the cruel equipment* of law: *from armed soldiers and cops, to guns, cannons, balls and chains, and prisons.* A law that, in the words of Luther Standing Bear, *designated not order but force and disorder.* They called the United States "Milahanskan," *the nation of long knives.*

———

The county condemns the land. The new bridge still spans the Fox River.

One winter, I stood under it and watched the water move, light glancing off the underside of the bridge's concrete piers. Birds had built nests where the underside of the road and piers meet, living beneath the jarring, hollow drone of semitruck tires. From the opposite bank of the Fox River, the house is an oddity, completely transparent except for its exterior columns. These are painted over with layers and layers of white paint so opaque and so matte that they seem to absorb light. They are reflected as white lines in the surface of the Fox River, reaching across but never touching the opposite bank where I sit.

Bone white. Ghost white. White. Breaking across the river that will eventually rise and destroy the house.

25.

There is an impossibility to sewing up the ends of one's life and leaving for a new one, though this is something women are often encouraged to do. When I left Portland, it was fast, almost secret. I feel the shame of it when I read Edith's letters to her sister, Marion, apologizing that she only had time to pack up before she left the country for good, moving to Italy: *I had expected to give you a ring when I was in Chicago, but the confusion of packing, disposing, sending off, dealing with shipping brokers, and contemplating the decidedly closed navigation on Lake Michigan was not conducive to telephone calls.*

What is the departure without goodbye? I had not been able to tell anyone that I was leaving except the friend with whom I had blown glass. She left work early, and we went to the bar near my apartment. When I told her, she looked at me like I'd slapped her.

She was the only person I could speak to without any performativity. The only person who had relayed the story of her engagement to me with this phrase *so then I realized this is happening* with a roll of her eyes and deep annoyance, the only person to be honest with me about how depressing it had been to give birth, to be a mother, *the first year it was like I no longer existed.* And yet between the two of us, we had no language for how to say goodbye.

After that, I didn't tell anyone. I simply stopped answering texts, excused myself as ill, or tired, or busy. Useless to two friends who were planning weddings. I sat on the floor of one friend's apartment, ate a fish that we had baked in parchment—ate it without silverware. How his fiancée, also my friend, returned home from work, furious at the piscine mess we had made. The watery hollow eye of the thing just stared up at the ceiling.

How much of it was my pride, how much was just the pursuit of, the love of, disappearing, of anonymity, of perpetual motion, of no fixed place or being. How much was the denial of beginnings and endings?

———

Edith puts an ad in the *Chicago Tribune* to sell the weekend house, described simply as a "77-foot-by-28-foot glass pavilion designed by Mies in 1950." On her sixty-fifth birthday, November 17, 1968, she buys an olive-green Fiat to be delivered to Naples. On December 13, 1968, in a small datebook in which little else is described, she writes, "Boarded M/V Italia." On the same day, she gets an international driver's permit, valid for one year. She sails to Italy and Greece. Her last note marked is January 18, 1969: Hotel Excelsior, Naples. She receives the car here.

All I have are the receipts I found in her collection at the Newberry—no narrative explanation, no goodbye. I cannot follow or re-create her footsteps, unable to trace this journey and too poor to afford a trip across Europe. My life will stand in as a poor substitute for hers: a broke college professor, beginning her life again, again. Sifting one life into another.

Death helps to mark things. The architect dies on August 17, 1969, in Chicago. His obituary, printed two days later in the *Chicago Tribune*, describes him as the architect of "glass house fame" but mentions specifically only the glass apartment buildings and other structures he built—not her house. It is as if he never built it.

———

I am pulling laundry out of the dryer when the friend who has recently gotten married calls to tell me that he's just been discharged from the hospital after a nervous breakdown, that he's okay, and that he's coming to visit. He stays for a week, sitting in the backyard all day drinking beer and studying another language, preparing for some future life. His eyes are brighter than they used to be, and I envy his project of translation, think of how it allows the possibility of multiple lives, multiple identities, of all the future rooms he has yet to inhabit. *You don't have to stay here*, he says, with frequency.

———

Among all of her papers, next to her international driver's permit of 1968, I find her brother's French driver's license from 1931. He's beautiful, just twenty years old, his black-and-white photograph stapled to a form. His address is 155 Boulevard du Montparnasse in Paris. This hotel still operates today, located between the Latin Quarter and Montparnasse. And yet, I can find no mention anywhere in her archive of her time here with Richard. Was he there during the period that she spent with Katharine and others on the Left Bank? Perhaps he refused to inherit the family business, to build on the family fortune; perhaps he left to find his own life. Perhaps she understood this better than anyone else in the family. Perhaps she encouraged it. Or perhaps I am once again playing the historian's game of projection.

Did she intentionally carry Richard's driver's license with her to Europe when she moved there again at the end of her life? I find their two licenses nestled together in a folder in her archive in a way that makes me want to believe that she carried her brother back with her.

———

I did not come to the desert with eyes prepared to see it. I drive between Santa Fe and Albuquerque for months, shocked at the expanse, the immensity. Eventually, I can read the immeasurable space, appreciate that from the highway I can watch a storm form in the sky miles away: the dark and distant clouds, the light that rakes through them to reveal the virga, streaks of rain that never touch down to the parched earth. The smell of rain, when it does come, is like the taste of blood—the deep minerality of it, the feeling of leaning against the rough adobe of the house during the monsoon season just to breathe this scent, like nothing I'd smelled before.

All translation begins with not knowing. Her translation of her life abroad required scaffolding, introducing, interlocuters who could assist. In the bundle of translations I receive back from Claudia, the Italian translator whose email address I have but whom I never meet, is a letter connecting Edith and poet Eugenio Montale. Elena Croce, daughter of philosopher Benedetto Croce, writes to Montale: *A friend of mine who you have already heard of, Edith Farnsworth, is here. She is a very intelligent woman, and I mean very intelligent— which is not something you see every day.* The casual sexism is grating . . . *she is most intimidated by you. She has just, for reasons of principle, quit her job as a doctor (which she had been doing, too, for reasons of principle), and being able to translate your work has really meant a lot to her. You should definitely meet her, either in Milan or Rome. How can we arrange this?*

This letter is a carbon copy. At the bottom, not typewritten but in handwriting, she addresses Edith directly: *And now, write to him saying: I'm coming.—Via Bighi 11 Milan, or look for him at the Senate (afternoons). Don't give up! Call me.*

Did she go? Did they meet? And if so, what transpired?

By October 1969, she writes (in English) a poem titled "Arsenio," Eugenio Montale's name for himself. It is written by hand—unusual for her—and imprinted with both month and year—also unusual. The specificity of these traces, the authenticity of them, is surprising to me.

Arsenio, you are my native tongue.
You are the trees among
Whose leaves my eyes are comforted.

You are the plants, the sands
The chasms into whose rocky hands
I fall
. . .
You are my land and sea, my language

This poem hints not at translation but at abandoning one life for another, *land, sea, language*. In this next chapter of her life, she becomes one of the first translators of Montale's work for English-speaking audiences. Perhaps this was a project of recall, as she'd lived in Italy for years in her youth. I find her practice work, her translations of Montale's *Xenia* (1966), which is a conversation the poet holds with his deceased wife.

For the hereafter we had worked out
a whistle, a sign of recognition.
I try to modulate it in the hope that we
are already dead and do not know it.

Montale wrote this one-way correspondence to his wife after her death, and these are the lines that Edith translated first. *Never did you think of leaving behind some trace of you in prose or verse.*

She spends hours—who knows how many—translating lines he has written for a woman who is not her, a woman who no longer exists.

———

I sift through folders of my Xeroxes of Edith's one-sided correspondence with her friends and family once she has moved to Italy. I place them on my colleague/landlord's deceased mother's desk in chronological order, facing the distant highway and more distant volcanoes. First, there are letters to her sister, then letters to Montale, then cards and letters from concerned friends—the recurring theme in these letters is that she is aging, and the recurring question in the few responses that she receives is whether she is still alive. I flip through photographs that I have taken of these letters.

Floral, lavender-, and cream-colored stationeries covered in the looping handwriting of the geriatric elite describing their lives: the second houses they can no longer afford to keep up, the precarity of inherited things, the falling apart of bodies. In my mind, I cannot erase the image of a chicken baked for so long that its tender flesh falls right off the bone. Look at *that*, my mother would say, carving knife in hand.

And yet, in every letter Edith writes, a new beginning is born. She seems to be constructing a persona, one that creates even more distance. Her letters to her sister begin on December 17, 1969, from Florence: she is selling the glass house to Lord Peter Palumbo. *The tariff is so high for the poor English who wish to export money that it isn't surprising that the affair has dragged on a bit.* The phrases are absolutely foreign to me: she is house hunting as she expects a windfall of money with this sale. *There is one house on the south slope of Fiesole which I am seriously interested in. I could close a good many rooms, particularly the chapel.*

———

One summer, I write a grant, cobble together a series of cheap flights, and visit this villa. Just outside of Florence, it is now a music school for children. There is a Xerox machine in the chapel, jammed against the wall underneath a plaster relief of cherubic angels. Two women, retired teachers who once worked here, walk me through the building; I am astonished at the palatial scale of it. We pause in the courtyard, and they point out the Medici family crest high up on a wall, evidence that this fourteenth-century villa belonged to someone in that sprawling political dynasty before Edith purchased it in the 1970s. From the top of the campanile, they explain the extents of what had been her property—acres of olive groves, farther than the eye can see—and we descend the tower and walk through the garden. We talk about her aging body, the endless rooms, and which ones she would have actually lived in: most likely those with access to the courtyard and the kitchen, we decide, where she could watch the three-legged tortoise that would frequent her garden.

These women have also done an extraordinary amount of research on Edith, both of them having moved to Italy in their forties, leaving behind lives that no longer fed them, beginning again.

———

She assures her sister that she has found love. *Perhaps you are wondering about the adorable Montale. The days working with him were absolutely lovely and we continue to exchange poetry. Imagine meeting your soul mate at my age! I'll try to write again. Love and best wishes.*

She writes that she is well, she is thriving, she is consuming, is buying and selling property, is translating poetry. There is no acknowledgment here of their ages: Marion is seventy, Edith is sixty-six; she doesn't ask any questions about their family members, she seems to have no curiosity about anyone—not Marion's husband or son. The unanswered letters become more and more extravagant in their detail. This is less a correspondence and more a script.

It isn't as if I haven't also lived like this at times, so centered on my own existence that I became an insatiable and empty void, a black hole.

The letters I have access to are the ones that Edith sent, that her sister kept and donated to the Newberry Library. I see none of the letters Marion wrote in response. Perhaps she didn't, as Edith was not really inviting conversation but rather describing her own life. *I am wondering if you received a letter from me*, Edith writes, *I have no word from you.*

In this one-way correspondence, there is the suspension of actual knowledge of the other, another potential mistranslation.

Some people can't handle this. Freud snaps when his fiancée does not respond immediately to his letters: this one-way monologue, he argues, will *make us strangers to each other when we meet again, so that we find things different from what, without realizing it, we imagined.*

Barthes puts it more elegantly: *Without a reply the other's image changes, becomes other.*

———

I'm not anyone's image of me anymore. I have a new morning routine: putting the kettle on to boil water for coffee and sweeping up the cockroach bodies while I wait, their threadlike legs touching their tender bellies, as if asleep. I take my new students on a walk in rural New Mexico during a field trip and miscalculate the distance between the highway and a distant tree, misjudge the terrain and lose them in the desert as they walk—I watch them, one by one, plunge below the horizon line because I had mistaken the desert for flat. I try to call out to them, the wind devouring my every word. The hard rain turns into hail. And then, hours later, all of us breathlessly collect at the tree, which is dead but holds a perfectly spherical, giant nest in it large enough for a human.

I visit the Valles Caldera, the healed-over wound of a dormant volcano. I stand in it, and it is so silent, so still that I can hear the movement of the clouds. Their language is a low hum in my chest.

My image has changed, become other, in this landscape large enough to swallow me whole.

26.

When I am alone in this environment, it shocks me back into the memory of summers in northeastern Nebraska—the expansiveness of the sky and its mirror image in the broad, yellow plains beneath it, immeasurable distances. Standing in the McDonald Ranch House on what is now the White Sands Missile Range, near Alamogordo, New Mexico, where scientists assembled the plutonium core for the first atomic bomb in a house they stole from ranchers, I drift to the window between rooms and stare out at the still-radioactive horizon, which looks like both death and home.

The atomic blast of the Trinity bomb sucked the desert floor upward into a fireball that rained down radioactive glass. This glass was given its own name, *trinitite*. Trinitite still litters the ground there. Although it is illegal to take trinitite from the site or to sell it, I hold it in my hand, tiny, jagged green-and-gray pieces. The man who has handed them to me tells me that it's perfectly fine to hold trinitite but warns me not to put it in my mouth.

We arrange the pieces on my desk in tiny constellations, and he explains

that the piece the size of my thumbnail, the one with the red streak in it, contains iron from the tower on which the bomb was perched when it detonated—remains of the tower live on in this glass. He lets me keep the smallest shards, and from time to time I take them out and put them over my photographs of her—something between a protective halo and a blossoming firework surrounding her head. She commissioned the glass house the same year this bomb was detonated in the desert to create this radioactive fallout, two kinds of glass.

FIGURE 18. *Glass Document II.*

I have come out just as if I had been among the dead to hear how bad things are among the living. She translates a line from an Albino Pierro poem into a tiny notebook full of such fragments—and it stings when I see it on the page, when I retype it on my laptop.

———

You can find confessions strung across the desert, open sores in the landscape. Most of them are narrativized as necessary advancements in science and technology. If you visit the site of the first nuclear bomb blast, although it is a felony, you will notice that every visitor has their eyes trained on the ground looking for little pieces of trinitite to steal. I already have one in my pocket, half hoping it will sterilize me and I will be rid of the threat of childbearing, another thing I can't afford. One of my students points in the direction of a man I recognize as the one who first showed me these minuscule glass shards. He is sitting cross-legged on the ground, scooping up the sand and dropping it in his mouth, eating mouthfuls of dirt laced with nuclear fallout in protest, as he does every year. We are all enclosed in an ordinary chain-link fence, a perfect circle of it that circumscribes where the ground was turned into radioactive, wormlike bubbles of green glass.

This fence is dotted with black-and-white photographs of the white scientists and generals responsible for polluting this place and all places that have been touched by nuclear experimentation—an exhibition of pure but unintended irony. Their pale faces hover over an expanse of land they destroyed in ways that have torn through skin and organs for generations.

There were many people living in proximity to the first atomic blast, and they thought the world was ending. The atomic bomb was an experiment stuffed with so much plutonium that for a fraction of a second it gave off heat 10,000 times greater than the surface of the sun. The unspent fallout went everywhere and rained down on children. Radioactive ash fell like snow, and they played in it, scooping it up in their hands, opening their mouths so that it could dance on the ends of their tongues.

Weeks after the blast, the U.S. military would invite a group of journalists from Iowa to stand in the glassy crater that was left, would encourage them to chip off pieces of the sparkling, radioactive fallout—*atomsite*, they called it, before changing its name to *trinitite* later—and bring it home to their wives and girlfriends to wear as jewelry. They told the men it was safe for women to adorn themselves but warned them not to put it in their own pockets because it could render them sterile. The people on whom the fallout fell, however, received no warning, no explanation.

The glint in Oppenheimer's eyes when he quotes a line from the Bhagavad Gita that, he claims, came to mind as he watched the desert being destroyed: *now I am become death, destroyer of worlds.*

But the Bhagavad Gita doesn't present death as death—it presents death as an illusion. We are not born and we do not die. It does not present the version of death that we are familiar with but death as "world-destroying time."

We each carry the legacy of this in our bodies. A radioactive carbon known as atmospheric 14 C doubled during nuclear weapons testing in the 1950s and 1960s, and we are still carrying evidence of this in our bodies. This is the Anthropocene, the world-destroying time.

A few people laughed, a few people cried, most were silent, Oppenheimer sniffs. In the recording of this speech, he looks skeletal, sick, a living calavera.

Now we are all sons of bitches fits better: the words of Kenneth Bainbridge.

I'm standing at the center of this history, at the center of this crater. Your body is somewhere beyond this, with other bodies. It is having its own experience. It is being moved beyond itself, it is encountering the sawtoothed fear of the incommunicable, as is mine. It is one of many future lamentations, as is mine, as are all living bodies.

———

Death turns us each into a character. As she neared death, she began to disclose parts of her past, to try to place the decisions she made in context and order, to make a story out of them, and a particular hero of herself.

Is the fact that her life in Italy is completely missing from her memoirs a sign that during this time, she is writing them? Tearing herself out of the present to order the events of the past?

You write about your life only if you are willing to show yourself while you were doing the living, or at least now that you are doing the remembering, she writes.

———

In a letter to her sister, she writes that she cannot deal with the climate of liberated sexuality of the 1970s. She complains about translating Albino Pierro's "Songbook of Love."

Poor Albino couldn't have tapped a drier source. I'm fed to the teeth with Marilyn Monroe, sex, nudes, and all the rest. I'd prefer to find a pair of leg-o-mutton sleeves than the endless, glossy photos of an umbilicus. Well, I'm struggling with the songbook.

But Marilyn would have died in 1962, a decade before this translation work began. And in death, Edith is still *fed to the teeth* with her image.

In photographs taken by George Barris just weeks before she died, Marilyn Monroe is on Santa Monica beach. It's late in the day, and she has the distant, glassy stare of a woman who's been drinking—I, too, have found myself in that space some days when it has felt necessary to put a gloss over life, to smooth out the edges. In some of her photos, she is wrapped in a large sweater and cringes against the cold while the ocean licks at her heels. It looks painful, and none of this escapes the camera's gaze.

The book of Pierro's "love songs" that Edith translates includes an introduction written by a man who writes that the "you" used by Pierro is not any individual or specific woman but instead, *an unfathomable "other"* who represents the *eternal feminine, prerational and premoral*, one that combines all *good and evil, joy and pain, tenderness and cruelty, fidelity and treachery. She has all the connotations of magic . . . superstition, fear and familiarity with the world of the dead and with that of animals.*

Edith carefully chooses the words that translate the meaning in Pierro's poems. And yet, she allows the poet to say to a woman he desires, *sew into your eyes the light of my own as they look at you.*

What does it mean to be trapped in this gaze? To have the light of another's eyes sewn into your own?

————

In a famous photograph described as "taken at the end of her marriage to Joe DiMaggio"—her body and time defined, as ever, by male occupation—Marilyn Monroe reads *Ulysses* in a bathing suit. "She has just begun dating Arthur Miller, and is trying to fit into his world," speculates a man in the comment section below the image, in that eternal present tense of the internet. She seems to have turned to the final chapter of the book, known as Molly Bloom's soliloquy. In this chapter, Molly—who is also, as a character, a rough translation of *The Odyssey*'s Penelope, and of Joyce's actual wife, Nora Barnacle, in that way in which women are often made into symptom or symbol of something they did not choose—is saying of her husband, *I thought well as well him as another*, and *I liked him because I saw he understood or felt what a woman is and I knew I could always get round him.*

But is Marilyn really reading this book? asks the internet. *A photograph of a woman reading a book indicates that the woman is reading that book*, writes the author of another comment.

I close this window.

———

Eve Arnold, who took this photograph, states that Marilyn drove around with this worn copy of *Ulysses* in her glove compartment. Her time with the famous actress reveals just a facet of what must have unfolded in Marilyn's mind—a mind having a life so different from and yet so familiar to all women because that mind existed in a body that the world has never ceased consuming. *Fed to the teeth*, writes Edith.

A woman's body and its presence—or an image of it—is seen as "sex." One afternoon, I delete the nudes that have mysteriously migrated from my phone to my laptop, toying with the idea of erasing everything on it, sending it back to my former institution, choosing the desert for good. The laptop is the only thing connecting me to it—the last piece of university infrastructure still in place. The dissolving boundaries of digital images means nothing is fixed. I have nightmares in which I am lecturing in an auditorium of students and the photos begin scrolling across the enormous projection screen.

It takes an expert to know how to erase anything that exists in the digital world because there's no longer any such thing as erasure. Every digital imprint is immortal. A friend of a friend tries to help me understand what it would take to erase everything.

How clean do you want the computer? Regular clean or government clean?

She explains that the "more clean" process merely means putting more 1's and 0's between the images and the ability to retrieve them, 1 and 0 being binary code for distance.

27.

Is it still a research relationship when you have read somebody else's memoirs so many times that they seem to become your own? When the language of these memories is so vivid that the images described in the text lodge in your mind not as language but as vision? I have read over and over her description of emerging from one of the tunnels along the autostrada in Rome, *at the season when the slopes and embankments beyond* the opening at the end of the tunnel *were blazing with the pure yellow of the broom which seemed to cover them completely.* I have read it so frequently that years later, when I moved to the desert where broom is everywhere, I thought I had seen it before, had experienced it already.

———

The collection of Albino Pierro poems that she translates is titled *Nu belle fatte*, Lucanian dialect for the Italian, *Una bella storia,* which is both *A Beautiful Story* and *A Beautiful History.* It is published in 1976. I hold it in my hand, so small I can almost close my fist around it. The cover is lavender. She is the translator—she has no space here to write what she thinks, nor did she take that space: someone else writes the introduction.

She carries the book, like a surrogate, and spits it out into the world. Kate Briggs writes that translating a sentence can take up a whole afternoon, and I try to imagine these slow days and how she spent them, the silence of inhabiting another's world, and then inhabiting your own like a shadow whose source you cannot identify.

How she became acquainted with Pierro, when she decided to translate his poems, is unclear. He was nominated for a Nobel Prize twice but, unlike Montale, never awarded one. How she found her way into this world of Nobel Prize–winning poets, why it was how she spent her final years, I do not know.

I only know that I myself felt more like a genius in the presence of men who are considered "genius" until I realized my thoughts were clearer when I was alone. In their presence, I thought a lot about being in their presence: the way this might have looked or sounded to others, as though being a shadow in a genius's life vivified me. It did not.

———

Italian is foreign to me, and I make mistakes in translation that are rooted in my desire for this to be a story of holes, openings, gaps. I make epic mistakes, publishing an article in which I claim that the title of this book was meant to be *occhiello*—the Italian word for "eyelet," a small hole or perforation—because I saw it, printed, on the first page of the proof that she marked up before publication.

Months after this article is published, I learn that *occhiello*, to her publisher, would simply have meant *blank page.*

I am delighted to learn this: a blank page, another opening. A history of love songs, as Pierro calls this book, would naturally contain some air.

———

Albino Pierro's return to writing in a Lucanian dialect is itself sprung from desire. This language bursts from him one evening as he rides the train back to Rome from his small hometown of Tursi, a moment of homesickness and regret for ever having left, for having become an academic (and one, in particular, who teaches history). Gianfranco Folena, who writes the introduction to this translation, describes this sudden shift in Pierro's writing toward his childhood dialect as a *real descent "dasuttaterre" (beneath the earth) . . . into the otherworld of the shattered realm of our history.*

Lucanian deviates from Italian, he writes, because it is *outside the course of history, as suitable for speaking to the dead as to the living.* Is this why she found it so compelling to translate?

———

An incomplete list of subjects in Pierro's *beautiful story* that also appear when the first nuclear blast on the planet tears across New Mexico:

The "pins of light" which blind
The wet rope which twists beneath the blazing sun and tongues of fire
The red pomegranate burst open and again blood
The cloud tinged pink by the sun
The dust and the wind

———

The high desert is a world of light: the sun reflected off the dusty ground, thin ribbons of shadow lying low beneath the vegetation. In the early fall, chamisa blossoms in bright golden clouds that seem to float just above the ground. When things should be dying, it comes to life. It ignites vast stretches of land between towns, and I ride the train for hours for no reason except to let the vision of it wash over me until I am unable to speak.

28.

The department chair at my new institution wants to make a postcard showing off the faces of the four women under forty that have just been hired, since they haven't hired women in years. We are meant to be flattered by this but sit in shock and silence in a meeting during this announcement. Instead, the school hires a film crew to simply follow around the youngest one of us for the entire day, pushing a camera in her face and telling her to *act as if she is teaching*. She's from Spain and is beautiful. From my neighboring studio, I hear her protest, *I am teaching; I don't understand.* They have her perform "teaching" for hours after the class ends, into the night. Her students are wary extras in this film, the lights the crew brought are melting everyone's faces off. *Once more*, I hear the all-male crew leader exclaim as I leave the building to head to the nearest bar and try to forget that this is my life now.

What are women, to this world?
And yet, this is the world I must live in.

———

I have not decided if I will stay in New Mexico, but I begin the process of forgetting my life before I came here, of distancing the past in order to make a logical decision. I drag files from my laptop to a hard drive and wait, watching the calculation of percentages and time. I spend many afternoons asking my computer to forget everything that has migrated into its memory.

I organize my previous life into folders, label the folders, and drag them onto new hard drives, blank islands of space. They come with their own factory-installed identities: PASSPORT and NO_NAME. I enclose each memory island in a hard-shell plastic case that would protect against humidity if I were ever to travel to a place with moisture in the air. The cases lock. I lock away research trips, syllabi, assignments, manuscript drafts. I lock away the intimate photographs I have taken of myself for various men. I lock away these former (untitled) versions of my body: on its side, in black, photographed from the tip of the nose to the rise of the left hip, left breast forming a pendulous moon; my shoulders and head rising out of the bathtub, the humidity curling my hair and softening my skin.

———

The correspondence between Edith and Montale is about both translations of poetry and the various failures of their bodies. To live is to die. Is this a translation from one bodily form to another?

Montale writes to her, from Rome on February 26, 1976, saying, *I wish I could write more clearly, but I can't.* He describes what initially drew him to her. It was her translation of Leopardi's "La ginestra," *the first of your beautiful translations that I came across*, he writes.

"La ginestra," written in 1836, is translated into English as "Wild Broom" or "The Flower of the Desert." Wild broom, Leopardi writes, is a flower that grows in the desert, a *lover of sad places abandoned by the world*, beautifying the very "emptiness" that will inevitably destroy it. The poet speaks directly to the broom. He tells it that when Vesuvius erupts again, it will accept its fate graciously:

> *you'll have been so much wiser*
> *so much less unsound than man, since you*
> *have never believed your frail species*
> *can be made immortal by yourself, or fate.*

As for humankind, which is the opposite of this wise plant, the metaphor he offers is an elaborately produced anthill crushed by a ripened apple falling from a tree.

––––––

The desert is the sun, the riddle of which Robert Smithson describes this way: *It was not a single flaming star but millions upon millions of them, all clustering thickly together like bees in a swarm.* The sun, he says, is not one *solid, impenetrable flame* but *innumerable suns.* The language we ordinarily use to describe time and space is puny and oriented mostly toward labor and acquisition. It isn't the landscape that is empty but us: we are close to nothing. We were all objects in the sun.

The desert opens up the enclosure of my body. The desert says, *You are not a body; you are part of the world* and wrenches its way in. And in this way, the desert has made me remember my body. On leaving for the East Coast, a friend I had made in the desert hugged me and said, *Whatever you do, don't die here.* But I wouldn't mind. If I die in the desert, she will make it fast; there will be no lingering. She will tear through my skin like paper.

Nothing I write can make Edith immortal or change the story of who she is, who she was, or what she has hidden from us; I can hold the shards of what I have found up to the light for you, let you see whatever glints off them. I cannot save her, cannot change her experience of the world, or make her better than she was, or better than human. Here, I would repeat her words: *I am not proud of the translation . . . But it is hoped that its curious and lovely quality may still be traceable through the metamorphosis.*

29.

After *Who did she fuck?* the question *How did she die?* seems to be the only concrete thing anyone wants to know—as if sex and death define us.

The man writing her biography is getting to the end, the end is death. He asks the glass house tour guides to email me questions like this and they do dutifully, a cluster of them landing in my inbox one day. It is as if instead of a writer, I am a ventriloquist: as if she could speak through me, as if behind my open mouth there is some original source.

I have tried that approach. On what I thought would be my last visit to her glass house, I wore a dress made in the 1940s, the same decade in which she began to talk about this project with the architect. I laid down in a bed that never belonged to her but stands in as hers. It was designed by the architect's grandson, and it participates in a patrilineal, artificial history of the house, rounding out the furniture that the architect designed but that never occupied the house with her.

I breathed in and out death. I walked to her kitchen, opening a few drawers and closing them. At the edge of the house outside, the elderly tour guide who had been sent down the hill to keep an eye on me fell into a game on her phone. I took the gin and dry vermouth (Edith's favorite) out of my backpack and mixed myself a martini. I sat in a chair that the architect designed, and I tried to draw out Edith's thoughts in pencil on paper. I even put the pencil in my left hand, as a friend suggested, in order to have as little control as possible. I traced just the fragments of letters on the page, barely forming words. It was supposed to be a séance, but when I put pencil to paper to do the automatic writing exercise, I just kept coming up with the words "you tell," and I did not know if it was the martini or the ghost speaking.

Although, chronologically, everything should compel me to write about her death, I find that the facts are too bare. She was weak. Perhaps osteoporosis? She writes to a few correspondents about snapped ribs. She is living in the villa she purchased near Florence. A young Italian family moves into the villa to take care of her. Someone has stolen the silver. The mail is too slow. She is out of her favorite typing paper. She spends days in the courtyard watching a lemon tree.

And then the letters simply stop.

I sit in my studio now, listening to the audio recording I made when I occupied her glass house. The sounds of my body, the sounds of my breath. My steps, too, which at times sound distant, though they were just five feet beneath the microphones in my ears. The sound of the weight of my body as it settled into a chair, the sound of mass against leather that wasn't warmed by my body but rubbed against it, unyielding. The slow sound of my breathing as I tried to fall asleep in the bed.

Could I consider this my attempt at a translation of her life? My body poured into hers, her autobiographical reflections glancing off my own? I listen to my hands moving as hers, touching the perfect white drapes, but this is just a proxy for the original. I am shorter than her, wider—could I be considered the perfect translator? I've always believed myself to be, have fashioned out of my life at least ten years to inhabit hers, if not twenty. When I explained this to a curator once, a man curious about my work, he took the news as if I'd just explained I had a terminal illness, horrified. *You've spent ten years of your life . . .* he shook his head. The way in which

FIGURE 19. *I Listened.*

a woman inhabiting another woman's world was viewed as an enormous waste of time, of my youth, of my life. I never hear from the curator again, the exhibition we were planning together vanished. What I could not, at that time, explain: that I see my life and Edith's as parallel projects, have found in her writing a way of making sense of my own life, a kind of relief.

30.

How is one to travel through a country without landmarks,
toward a destination so attenuated
as nearly to be forgotten?

There is a row of posts, but not a fence and
not a field.
Now looms the shadow of a maple tree, without a landscape.
On the right you see a mailbox—Hoskins is the name
—And soon another, with the name J. Humphrey.
No farmhouse is there to be seen;
for the names, no bearer.

The first time I read her poem "February Thaw," I imagined her driving to the house on rural roads buried under weeks of snow, a bleak, white expanse with no beginning and no end. Now when I read it, I think of the weeks that stretch behind me and in front of me.

I avoid all human contact. I go to the grocery store once a month, stock supplies, truss a whole chicken with dental floss because I cannot find any twine. On the cold, gray afternoons of this strange early spring, I let the high desert wind throw dust in my face on long walks in the forest that follows the Rio Grande, a place at the edge of my neighborhood. I look for signs of life. The geese have become territorial, seeing so few humans now that they sense something weak or sick about me as I approach with my mask on. They make me walk around them on the trail, watch me warily, necks and wings outstretched.

When I return to the house after these long, bleak walks, I smell my grandmother's and mother's cooking: roasted chicken, bones and vegetable scraps boiling for hours to make broth, the scent of the chocolate cake that I bake for myself (and will later eat with my bare hands, out of the pan), shallots caramelized in butter. Alone for weeks, I have somehow taken refuge in their cooking, though I always resisted learning it.

Cream-colored Bruno Mathsson chaise lounges with laminated beechwood and woven hemp straps. Jens Risom chairs made of discarded parachute webbing from World War II. Two slipper chairs custom-made to replicate the simple pair that flanked Edith's fireplace when she lived here— produced in China, these were seized by U.S. customs and observed and tested, our awareness of the new virus being so xenophobic that not even inanimate objects were spared. I had been working closely with the National Trust for Historic Preservation for years to present the house as Edith had actually lived in it, furnished with pieces from the woman-owned Chicago furniture store Baldwin Kingrey. Overnight, the house was put into an institutional freeze.

The furniture sits in the house, waiting behind glass for the virus to stop. I am relieved by this fact. I cannot resolve entering this structure inhabited by replicas of her furniture because to do so might suggest some sort of closure, an acceptance of a cycle of history suddenly made just. This justice arrives so late that I don't want to witness it and accept it, to put aside the

FIGURE 20. Installation view of *Edith Farnsworth, Reconsidered*.

silence of so many years in which she did not seem to exist. I cannot decide which is worse: a house full of the architect's furniture, which pretends that this was always his house, that he lived here; or a house full of approximations of her furniture, an impossible fantasy that she is still here. Something is lost in the re-creation, something violent in that her words do not live here, nor does her voice. Just reproductions of things that were long-ago destroyed when the river rose over its banks.

In the only review of this exhibition that I believe does her any justice, the writer describes her as *mysterious* and leaves it at that: she cannot be understood or conjured out of the objects we have placed in the house.

Months later, I decide to see it for myself. I head to Illinois, driving north from Albuquerque. There is still no vaccine. The sun stays tethered to my windshield for hours, blinding me.

How is one to travel through a country without landmarks,
toward a destination so attenuated
as nearly to be forgotten?

FIGURE 21. Installation view of *Edith Farnsworth, Reconsidered.*

The sun flattens the earth, igniting the mute colors of the desert brush. Shaggy junipers, the tangled gray stems and ocher flower heads of chamisa, and spiny shoots of chollas and ocotillos stretch to the horizon on either side of the highway, all of them on fire with the sunset, drinking in the light.

When the sun sets, it is as if the world I know has burned away. What's left is a black void through which I follow taillights down rural roads, trying to find the small house I rented through Airbnb in a tiny town in Colorado, trying to stick to the edges, low-density places that I believe are safer. I weave through a small town, afraid to stop, a lone woman in rural Colorado with New Mexico license plates. I pull into a parking lot to pee into a disposable cup, too afraid to use the public restroom in a gas station where not even the attendants are masked. I unroll the window to let the urine stream out of the cup and down the highway, careful to angle it so that the force of air doesn't send it back into my face.

When I arrive to my destination, I put on my mask and latex gloves. It takes me thirty minutes to unload all the food I will eat over two weeks— the coolers of perishables, the bins of dry goods and wine. When Edith went to the glass house, she would go through a similar process. Living in the house on Wednesdays and weekends meant constant unpacking and packing, the *eerie solitude* of the drive from her apartment in Chicago to the glass house in Plano, Illinois.

I drive to Omaha next, the place I was born, which always feels like returning to the first sentence of a book I put down too soon, a book I always wanted to finish but never will. The distance between my body and the bodies of my parents is something I can feel when I see them through the glass of the front door—they keep their masks on at first, my father at the top of the stairs, his hands in his pockets, my name muffled through two layers of fabric as he says it. My mother hugs me. I can feel that she is holding her breath. I have to remind them three times that I have quarantined for two weeks, that I have tested negative, that I haven't been in any indoor public places at all.

They take their masks off and we have dinner, but they continue to look at me as if I am something new to them, their eyes wide. Perhaps mine are, too. It is seven months into the stay-at-home order, and the concept of family is now strange, the once-familiar feeling of our skin pressed together as we hug goodbye now tinged with fear.

Instead of projecting the family line forward, instead of producing children, I am always casting backward, trying to reclaim the strange women that I am descended from, to bring them into the present with me. I leave Nebraska with the pony coat my great-aunt wore packed into the trunk, splayed over the top of all of my provisions, heavy, like it still contains her body or the pony's body.

I drive with this skinned thing in my trunk, pouring my urine out the window the whole way to Illinois. I wonder if this makes me insane.

Despite this, autumn perfumes the air with the familiar sweet smell of decay that announces the change in seasons.

The house looks as if she never left. As if the river never rose to destroy all of her furniture, to soak the curtains and make them absolutely filthy. It waits as if she were never served that summons that began to fray her life at the edges. As if she still lives here. As I approach, I can see furniture that she chose for this house, the delicate lines of a Florence Knoll table and chaise lounges. I see the slipper chairs, low to the ground, the stack of firewood that would make a perfect fire this afternoon, if such a thing were allowed.

When I step inside, I see that the dining table is set with white saucers and plates; a steel-plated coffee urn is on the table, one my mother chose for this exhibit.

For years, the house was suspended in time, and it took us with it—a period during which I disinfected groceries, washing even apples and lemons with hot water and dish soap, prematurely rotting them. We all held our breath. The house and each one of us, waiting, the kind of pause that happens between speaking words, or turning a page in silence.

But I am here now. And the body is still a body. I slip on the pony coat and I stand next to the house. I want to feel the weight of being trapped outside of the glass house in an animal skin, to bring my great-aunt, another woman who embraced solitude, to this place. It is heavy, and I don't know the name of it, don't know what she called it, this hide, but I feel it sinking me. I allow the coat to give me a different gravity, gestures that are not mine, to let it double me over. I find myself in the large black space under

FIGURE 22. *Equine in Features.*

the house. I kneel where her poodle grazed on the blood-clotted skulls of birds that had flown into the glass, letting my hide get covered in mud. I do not have to be precious with this body; it is borrowed, I am wearing something that already knows death, that doesn't fear endings any longer.

It feels alive when I am in it. In the distance, the boom-crack of men hunting. I walk a distance from the house and lay face down in the yellow-orange leaves, my heart pounding. I close my eyes, letting the coat cover everything but my hands and my face. I leave these out, naked in the cold air. When I see the photograph I took, I see how the ground has swallowed me whole.

Here is how I know that time is space, not chronology: I later learn that Edith once drove past a neighboring field to find it full of horses that had been shot dead—their gentle bodies bleeding out on the grass. Another story that never resolves, another gap in knowledge. She began to keep a rifle at the house.

———

It is easy to write about someone who is no longer alive. They cannot defend themselves, cannot argue. But it is also heartbreaking: a distance that cannot be collapsed. And there is no tidy resolution to it. Her life has already ended. Where does the writing end?

Even her memoirs end by refuting an ending: *I must have dreaded the full appearance, the fait accompli, a something limiting, something final, leading to the irremediable conclusion.*

Tomorrow, her furniture will be carried out of the house, padded, and crated. All of it will be shipped back to donors, companies, various spaces of storage. Tomorrow, I will drive west, return to New Mexico, to my life. It is the only life I will inhabit. The gravity of another person's life will no longer shelter, tether, or orient me, for better or for worse.

The sun is descending into the river. It glances off the white-painted steel of the house as it sets, making the structure blinding white while the long, blue shadows of trees snake into the interior of the house, just behind the glass. I am alone here, have been entrusted with the key. It feels inappropriate to call her *her* as I'm standing in her house with a high-definition video camera. She is also *you.*

What can I tell you? Perhaps that I arrived too late today to record this properly. That I thought filling your house with these re-creations could bring you to life. That, instead, as I stand here, your poems and translations run through me. *The wind has left you a clear echo / a quivering and thin line of sun.*

I see my own reflection in the same glass that once held yours. Nothing else here is the same. The curtains move as if breathing. The only light comes from the sunset, a burst that is fading. I never stop moving, viewing the house only through the lens of my camera. Trying, as best I can, not to exist so that I can, at last, see it through your eyes—a slice of setting sun that slides across the room, hovering for a moment just above the fireplace, the glow through the curtains as the day ends, the shiver of trees beyond the glass and the piles of leaves swirling in the wind, brittle and exploding into dust before my eyes.

I close the door behind me, step outside. Someone wrote, *The sun's mane was tangling. . . . The day gave out no sound.* You translated it from Italian into English years ago, and I watch this vision unfold. I film the house from the meadow. Standing in the frigid cold, I watch as the house dissolves into fragments of your poems marked by your own misgivings about language, about meaning.

^ *you are silent*
You are silent
                    Speechless
     you lie there with the body,   ^ *in unrelieved*
                    desperate and

     ^ *indifference*
     Indifferent.

                    the houses

are   women
are women   everything is
what it is is what it is.

House is a memory I reached on foot.

Acknowledgments

This book has been in progress for at least ten years and exists because of an incredible community of family, friends, collaborators, and teachers. All of my love and gratitude to the following: Alexis Smith, whose unparalleled friendship and generous reads, insightful edits, reading recommendations, and encouragement over many years made this book possible—you are my ideal reader. My incredible editor, Martha Bayne, who saw this book through many drafts and championed this project to the end, and Keia Mastrianni, who introduced us. Claire Potter, whose editorial insights helped this book find its final form. Alice T. Friedman, without whose work I could never have begun mine and whose friendship sustained me through this process. Laurence Sarrazin, whose collaborations on glassblowing inspired this book. Isabelle Loring Wallace, whose friendship and influence on how I see and write about contemporary art are gifts. Mitchell Squire, whose art, mentorship, and friendship continue to have a profound impact on me. The family of Edith B. Farnsworth, particularly her nephew, Fairbank Carpenter, who was a supportive and rich source for this history, and his wife, Lynne Carpenter, and their family: Robin Chestek, George Carpenter, Amy Fiore, Laura Miklautsch, and John Carpenter, who so generously gave their permission for Farnsworth's memoirs, correspondence, poetry, and photographs to appear in this book. Brennan Gerard and Ryan Kelly, whose friendship and art practice transformed my thinking. Christiana Langenberg, Debra Marquart, sheri crider and Barbara Bell, Brian Goldstein and Theresa McCulla, Aaron Cayer and Fernando Pichardo, Amanda Curreri and Welly Fletcher, Theaster Gates, Stephen Salazar and Sean Pavlik,

Charlie Vinz, Eric Allix Rogers, Juan Heredia, David L. Hays, Jonathan D. Solomon, Stephen Geering, Ted Jojola, Kevin Harrington, Linda Samuels, Maggie Grimason, Paul Lisicky, Renee Gladman, Melinda Frame, Kathy Kambic, Katya Crawford, Kristen Shaw, Nina Elder, Erin Elder, Nancy Zastudil, Marjorie Devon, Mira Woodson, Josh Stuyvesant, Jason Asenap, Cactus Eddie, Marty Pfeiffer, Andrea Packard, Tess Wei, and Viviette Hunt and Eric Sirotkin, who all held space for me and for this book in so many important ways as I researched, workshopped, and wrote it. Scott Mehaffey, for our collaborations at the Farnsworth House, many conversations, and a cherished friendship. Sue Sacharski, for invaluable and generous research help and instincts. Alison Hinderliter at the Newberry Library for her expert guidance in navigating contacts and archives. The remarkable research staff at the Newberry Library, Museum of Modern Art, Art Institute of Chicago, Canadian Centre for Architecture, and Castine Historical Society for critical support over many years. The Tin House Workshop, the Hambidge Center, the Santa Fe Art Institute, and the Swarthmore College List Gallery for the space to nurture this work. The University of New Mexico and my colleagues for the sabbatical support to complete this project.

I owe the greatest thanks to my parents, Jean Guinan Wendl and John Wendl (1953–2024), and my brother, Bill Wendl, for a lifetime of unconditional love, support, and laughter. And to Rick McKnight, for everything.

References

Poems (In order of appearance in book)

Soften these stones . . . , fragment of Albino Pierro, "When I Was a Child," trans. Edith B. Farnsworth

I looked about me . . . , fragment of Albino Pierro, "U Mamone," trans. Edith B. Farnsworth

Of spring burning in falling sentences . . . , fragment of Edith B. Farnsworth, "Night Drifts"

The wind has left you a clear echo . . . , fragment of Sandro Penna, "Autumno," trans. Edith B. Farnsworth

And I open my eyes . . . , fragment of Albino Pierro, "You Know It," trans. Edith B. Farnsworth

Eyes rimmed with salt or rimmed with light . . . , fragment of Edith B. Farnsworth, untitled poem

I envision endless space beyond . . . , fragment of Giacomo Leopardi, "L'infinito," trans. Edith B. Farnsworth

(Space is dark, windless, leafless and unblooming . . . , fragment of Edith B. Farnsworth, "Arsenio"

No, I won't add more wood . . . , fragment of Giorgio Bassani, "Epitaffio," trans. Edith B. Farnsworth

I woke . . . , fragment of Edith B. Farnsworth, "Artifact"

Is it time . . . , fragment from Edith B. Farnsworth, "Is It Time . . . "

"J'accuse," Edith B. Farnsworth

When shall I pick the long-loved moon . . . , fragment of Edith B. Farnsworth, "Images of Love"

I want to leave my bike . . . , fragment of Edith B. Farnsworth "Boy, Seventeen"

Now everything is getting to move slowly . . . , fragment in Farnsworth's journal, source unknown

Who knows what lies below? . . . , fragment of Albino Pierro, "Who Knows?" trans. Edith B. Farnsworth
Arsenio, you are my native tongue . . . , fragment of Edith B. Farnsworth, "Arsenio"
For the hereafter we had worked out a whistle . . . , fragment of Eugenio Montale, "Xenia," trans. Edith B. Farnsworth
I have come out just as if I had been among the dead . . . , fragment of Albino Pierro, unknown poem, trans. Edith B. Farnsworth
sew into your eyes . . . , fragment of Albino Pierro, "Come Quickly," trans. Edith B. Farnsworth
you'll have been so much wiser . . . , fragment of Giacomo Leopardi, "La ginestra," trans. Edith B. Farnsworth
How is one to travel . . . , fragment of Edith B. Farnsworth, "February Thaw"
The sun's mane was tangling . . . , fragment of "In the Void," unknown poet
^ you are silent . . . , fragments of Albino Pierro, "I vigliotte," and various others

Works Consulted

Arey, Leslie B. *Northwestern University Medical School 1859–1979: A Pioneer in Educational Reform*; A Revision and Extension of the 1959, Centennial Edition. Evanston, Illinois: Northwestern University, 1979.

Augustine of Hippo. *Confessions.* Translated by Maria Boulding. Hyde Park, NY: New City Press, 1997.

Douglas, Anne. "Dinner in Yesterday's Bedroom—It's Possible with This Flexible Plan." *Chicago Tribune*, August 24, 1952.

The Concise New Partridge Dictionary of Slang and Unconventional English. Edited by Tom Dalzell and Terry Victor. New York: Routledge, 2015.

"Ex-Owner of Mies-Created Farnsworth House Dies." *Chicago Tribune*, December 14, 1977.

Finfer, June. "The Glass House." 2010.

Farnsworth, Edith, et al. *Passavant Memorial Hospital General Information and Rules for Guidance of the House Staff and Clerks.* Chicago: Passavant Memorial Hospital, 1955.

Farnsworth, Edith. "The Poet and the Leopards." *Northwestern Triquarterly*, Fall 1960.

Graff, Rebecca S. "Edith Farnsworth House Site Report: An Investigation into the Archaeology of the Fox River Valley." 2022.

Kendall County vs. Mae C. Feeney, Edith B. Farnsworth, et al., 1968.

McFeatters, Ann. "Fox River Bridge Issue to Be Settled by Court." *Chicago Tribune*, May 2, 1968.

"Mies van der Rohe, 83, Architect of 'Glass House' Fame, Is Dead." *Chicago Tribune*, August 19, 1969.

Mies van der Rohe's Farnsworth House. Chicago: Towers Productions and Landmarks Illinois, 2008.

Montale, Eugenio. *Provisional Conclusions.* Translated by Edith B. Farnsworth. Chicago: Henry Regnery, 1970.

Pierro, Albino. *Nu belle fatte (Una bella storia; A Beautiful Story)*. Translated by Edith B. Farnsworth. Milan: Pesce d'Oro, 1976.

Quasimodo, Salvatore. *To Give and to Have, and Other Poems*. Translated by Edith B. Farnsworth. Chicago: Henry Regnery, 1969.

Sabatino, Michelangelo. *The Edith Farnsworth House: Architecture, Preservation, Culture*. New York: Monacelli Press, 2024.

Schulze, Franz, and Edward Windhorst. *Mies van der Rohe: A Critical Biography, New and Revised Edition*. Chicago: University of Chicago Press, 2012.

"Society Section." *Chicago Tribune*, February 1, 1942.

van der Rohe vs. Farnsworth, 1951.

Works and Exhibitions of Architecture Consulted

Edith Farnsworth, Reconsidered. Farnsworth House. Plano, Illinois, 2020–22.

Johnson, Philip. The Glass House. New Canaan, Connecticut, 1949.

Mies van der Rohe, Ludwig. Farnsworth House. Plano, Illinois, 1951.

Mies van der Rohe, Ludwig. Lake Shore Drive Apartments. Plano, Illinois, 1951.

Mies van der Rohe, Ludwig. McCormick House. Elmhurst, Illinois, 1952.

Mies van der Rohe, Ludwig. *Mies van der Rohe*, Museum of Modern Art. New York, New York, September 16, 1947–January 25, 1948.

Reich, Lilly, and Ludwig Mies van der Rohe. *Glasraum*, Werkbund exhibition "Die Wohnung." Stuttgart, Germany, 1927.

Yamasaki, Minoru. The World Trade Center Towers. New York, New York, 1973–2001.

Yamasaki, Minoru. Wendell O. Pruitt Homes and William Igoe Apartments Complex. Saint Louis, Missouri, 1954–72.

National Historic Landmarks and National Parks Consulted

Trinity Test Site, White Sands Missile Range. Socorro County, New Mexico.

Valles Caldera National Preserve. Jemez Springs, New Mexico.

White Sands National Park, New Mexico.

Works of Art Consulted

Ader, Bas Jan. *Broken Fall (Geometric)*. 1971.

Ader, Bas Jan. *Fall 1*. 1970.

Ader, Bas Jan. *In Search of the Miraculous*. 1975.

De Maria, Walter. *Mile Long Drawing*. 1968.

De Maria, Walter. *The Lightning Field*. 1977.

Dürer, Albrecht. *Draughtsman Making a Perspective Drawing of a Reclining Woman*. c. 1600.

Furuhashi, Teiji. *Lovers*. 1995.

Gerard, Brennan, and Ryan Kelly. *Modern Living*. 2016–present.

Manglano-Ovalle, Iñigo. *Le baiser/The Kiss*. 1999.

Moe, Ledelle. *Memorial (Collapse)*. 2005.
Smithson, Robert. *Spiral Jetty* [film]. 1970.
Squire, Mitchell. *OUT FROM*. 2020–21.
Starling, Simon. *Autoxylopyrocycloboros*. 2006.
Weams, Carrie Mae. "Kitchen Table" series. 1990.
Weams, Carrie Mae. *Roaming*. 2006.
Williamson, Marisa. "The Hemings Foundation" project. 2013–present.

Interviews Consulted

Barbara London in conversation with Teiji Furuhashi, 1994.
Edward Austin Duckett in conversation with Kevin Harrington, 1996. Canadian Centre for Architecture.
George Danforth in conversation with Kevin Harrington, 1996. Canadian Centre for Architecture.
Myron Goldsmith in conversation with Kevin Harrington, 1996. Canadian Centre for Architecture.

Collections Consulted

The Art Institute of Chicago, Ryerson and Burnham Library, Edward A. Duckett Collection (1931–78)
Canadian Centre for Architecture, Myron Goldsmith fonds (1933–96)
Ferenc M. Szasz Collection, University of New Mexico Center for Southwest Research
Library of Congress, Ludwig Mies van der Rohe Papers (1921–69)
Museum of Modern Art, The Ludwig Mies van der Rohe Archive
Newberry Library, Midwest MS Collections, Edith Farnsworth Papers (1900–1977)
Northwestern Memorial Hospital Archives, Edith Farnsworth, MD, papers (1938–77)

Writing I Think With

Ahmed, Sara. *Complaint!* Durham, NC: Duke University Press, 2021.
Ahmed, Sara. *Living a Feminist Life*. Durham, NC: Duke University Press, 2017.
Ahmed, Sara. *Queer Phenomenology: Orientations, Objects, Others*. Durham, NC: Duke University Press, 2006.
Banham, Reyner. *Scenes in America Deserta*. London: Thames & Hudson, 1982.
Barthes, Roland. *A Lover's Discourse: Fragments*. Translated by Richard Howard. New York: Hill and Wang, 1979.
Barthes, Roland. *Camera Lucida: Reflections on Photography*. Translated by Richard Howard. Reprint, New York: Hill and Wang, 2010.
Baudrillard, Jean. *Simulacra and Simulations*. Ann Arbor: University of Michigan Press, 1994.

Beal, Justin. *Sandfuture*. Cambridge, MA: MIT Press, 2021.

Benjamin, Walter. "Experience and Poverty." In *Walter Benjamin: Selected Writings Volume 2, Part 2, 1931–1934*, edited by Michael W. Jennings, Howard Eiland, and Gary Smith. Translated by Rodney Livingstone et al. Cambridge, MA: Belknap Press, 2002.

Benjamin, Walter. "On Scheerbart." In *Walter Benjamin: Selected Writings Volume 4, 1938–1940*, edited by Howard Eiland and Michael W. Jennings. Translated by Rodney Livingstone et al. Cambridge, MA: Belknap Press, 2003.

Benjamin, Walter. "On the Concept of History." In *Walter Benjamin: Selected Writings Volume 4, 1938–1940*, edited by Howard Eiland and Michael W. Jennings. Translated by Rodney Livingstone et al. Cambridge, MA: Belknap Press, 2003.

Bennett, Claire-Louise. *Pond*. Reprint, New York: Riverhead Books, 2017.

Bloomer, Jennifer. *Architecture and the Text: The (S)crypts of Joyce and Piranesi*. New Haven: Yale University Press, 1993.

Bloomer, Jennifer. "The Matter of Matter: A Longing for Gravity." In *The Sex of Architecture*, edited by Diana Agrest, Patricia Conway, and Leslie Kanes Weisman. Chicago: Harry N. Abrams, 1996.

Boyer, Anne. *A Handbook of Disappointed Fate*. New York: Ugly Duckling Presse, 2018.

Boyer, Anne. *Garments Against Women*. Boise: Ahsahta Press, 2015.

Briggs, Kate. *This Little Art*. London: Fitzcarraldo Editions, 2017.

Brodie, Janet Farrell. *The First Atomic Bomb: The Trinity Site in New Mexico*. Lincoln: University of Nebraska Press, 2023.

Cadwell, Michael. *Strange Details*. Cambridge, MA: MIT Press, 2007.

Carson, Anne. *Red Doc>*. Reprint, New York: Vintage, 2014.

Derrida, Jacques. *Geneses, Genealogies, Genres, and Genius: The Secrets of the Archive*. Translated by Beverley Bie Brahic. Edinburgh: Edinburgh University Press, 2006.

Ebeling, Siegfried. *Space as Membrane*. Translated by Pamela Johnston. Edited by Spyros Papapetros. London: Architectural Association London, 2010.

Emerling, Jae. *Photography: History and Theory*. New York: Routledge, 2011.

Estes, Nick. *Our History Is the Future: Standing Rock versus the Dakota Access Pipeline, and the Long Tradition of Indigenous Resistance*. New York: Verso, 2019.

Faderman, Lillian. *Odd Girls and Twilight Lovers: A History of Lesbian Life in 20th-Century America*. Reprint, New York: Columbia University Press, 2012.

Fleischmann, T. *Syzygy, Beauty: An Essay*. Louisville: Sarabande Books, 2011.

Forty, Adrian. *Words and Buildings: A Vocabulary of Modern Architecture*. London: Thames and Hudson, 2004.

Friedman, Alice T. "In this cold barn we dream." *Art Bulletin* 76, no. 4 (1994): 575–78.

Friedman, Alice T. *Women and the Making of the Modern House: A Social and Architectural History*. New Haven: Yale University Press, 2007.

Gallop, Jane. *Feminist Accused of Sexual Harassment*. Durham, NC: Duke University Press, 1997.

Gladman, Renee. *Calamities.* Seattle: Wave Books, 2016.

Gómez, Myrriah. *Nuclear Nuevo México: Colonialism and the Effects of the Nuclear Industrial Complex on Nuevomexicanos.* Tucson: University of Arizona Press, 2022.

Hagberg, Eva. *When Eero Met His Match: Aline Louchheim Saarinen and the Making of an Architect.* Princeton: Princeton University Press, 2022.

Hartman, Saidiya. "Venus in Two Acts." *Small Axe* 12, no. 2 (2008): 1–14.

Hartman, Saidiya. *Wayward Lives, Beautiful Experiments: Intimate Histories of Riotous Black Girls, Troublesome Women, and Queer Radicals.* New York: Norton, 2019.

Hathaway, Katharine Butler. *The Journals and Letters of the Little Locksmith.* New York: Coward-McCann, 1946.

Hathaway, Katharine Butler. *The Little Locksmith: A Memoir.* New York: Feminist Press, 2000.

Haushofer, Marlen. *The Wall.* Translated by Shaun Whiteside. New York: New Directions, 2022.

Hu, Tung-Hui. *A Prehistory of the Cloud.* Cambridge, MA: MIT Press, 2016.

Joyce, James. *Ulysses.* New York: Vintage Books, 1986.

Kraus, Chris. *I Love Dick.* Los Angeles: Semiotext(e), 1997.

Léger, Nathalie. *Suite for Barbara Loden.* Translated by Natasha Lehrer and Cécile Menon. Saint Louis, MO: Dorothy, a publishing project, 2016.

Lispector, Clarice. *The Hour of the Star.* Translated by Benjamin Moser. New York: New Directions, 2020.

Manguso, Sarah. *The Two Kinds of Decay: A Memoir.* London: Picador, 2009.

Moten, Fred, and Stefano Harney. *The Undercommons: Fugitive Planning & Black Study.* London: Minor Compositions, 2013.

Nelson, Maggie. *Bluets.* Seattle: Wave Books, 2009.

Nelson, Maggie. *Jane: A Murder.* Reissue ed. New York: Soft Skull Press, 2016.

Nelson, Maggie. *The Argonauts.* Minneapolis: Graywolf Press, 2016.

Nelson, Maggie. *The Red Parts: A Memoir.* New York: Free Press, 2007.

Neumeyer, Fritz. *The Artless Word: Mies van der Rohe on the Building Art.* Translated by Mark Jarzombek. Cambridge, MA: MIT Press, 1994.

Offill, Jenny. *Dept. of Speculation.* New York: Knopf, 2014.

Offill, Jenny. *Weather: A Novel.* New York: Knopf, 2020.

Ortega y Gasset, José. *History as a System and Other Essays toward a Philosophy of History.* Rev. ed. Translated by Helene Weyl. New York: Norton, 1962.

Ortega y Gasset, José. *On Love: Aspects of a Single Theme.* Translated by Toby Talbot. Eastford, CT: Martino Fine Books, 2012.

Perec, Georges. *Species of Spaces and Other Pieces.* Translated by John Sturrock. London: Penguin, 2008.

Piper, Adrian. *Escape to Berlin: A Travel Memoir.* Berlin: APRA Foundation Berlin, 2018.

Preciado, Paul. "Mi(E)s Conception: The Farnsworth House and the Mystery of the Transparent Closet." Translated by Keith Harris. *Society and Space*, November

4, 2019. https://www.societyandspace.org/articles/mies-conception-the
-farnsworth-house-and-the-mystery-of-the-transparent-closet.

Quetglas, Josep. *Fear of Glass: The German Pavilion in Barcelona.* Translated by J. Stone and R. Roig. Basel: Birkhäuser, 2001.

Rankine, Claudia. *Citizen: An American Lyric.* Minneapolis: Graywolf Press, 2014.

Scheerbart, Paul, and Bruno Taut. *Glass Architecture and Alpine Architecture.* New York: Praeger, 1972.

Scheerbart, Paul. *Lesabéndio: An Asteroid Novel.* Translated by Christina Svendsen. Cambridge, MA: Wakefield Press, 2012.

Schirren, Matthias. *Bruno Taut: Alpine Architektur: Ein Utopie, A Utopia.* New York: Prestel Verlag, 2004.

Sennett, Richard. "Plate Glass." In *Raritan Reading,* edited by Richard Poirier, 351–63. New Brunswick, NJ: Rutgers University Press, 1990.

Shapland, Jenn. *My Autobiography of Carson McCullers.* Portland, OR: Tin House Books, 2020.

Stegner, Wallace. *All the Little Live Things.* New York: Viking, 1967.

Stein, Gertrude. "Miss Furr and Miss Skeene." *Vanity Fair,* July 1923.

Stewart, Susan. *Poetry and the Fate of the Senses.* Chicago: University of Chicago Press, 2001.

Vuong, Ocean. *On Earth We're Briefly Gorgeous.* London: Penguin, 2019.

Waldrop, Rosmarie. *Lavish Absence: Recalling and Rereading Edmond Jabès.* Middletown, CT: Wesleyan University Press, 2002.

Walsh, Joanna. *Break.up.* Los Angeles: Semiotext(e), 2018.

White, Hayden V. *The Practical Past.* Evanston, IL: Northwestern University Press, 2014.

Williams, Terry Tempest. *When Women Were Birds: Fifty-Four Variations on Voice.* New York: Picador, 2013.

Woolf, Virginia. *A Room of One's Own.* Boston: Mariner Books, 2005.

Zambreno, Kate. *Drifts: A Novel.* New York: Riverhead Books, 2020.

Zamyatin, Yevgeny. *We.* Reprint, New York: Modern Library, 2006.

Writing I Think Against

Anon. "Houses: Architect & Client." *Architectural Forum: The Magazine of Building,* October 1951.

Barry, Joseph A. "Report on the Battle between Good and Bad Modern Houses." *House Beautiful,* May 1953.

Barry, Joseph A. "The Emperor's New Palace." *House Beautiful,* May 1953.

Beam, Alex. *Broken Glass: Mies van der Rohe, Edith Farnsworth, and the Fight over a Modernist Masterpiece.* New York: Random House, 2020.

Gordon, Elizabeth. "The Threat to the Next America." *House Beautiful,* April 1953.

Kelsky, Karen. *The Professor Is In: The Essential Guide to Turning Your Ph.D. into a Job.* New York: Crown, 2015.

Kinsey, Alfred C., Wardell B. Pomeroy, Clyde E. Martin, and Paul H. Gebhard. *Sexual Behavior in the Human Female*. Philadelphia: W. B. Saunders, 1953.

Schulze, Franz. *Mies van der Rohe: A Critical Biography*. Chicago: University of Chicago Press, 1985.

Illustration Credits

Figure 1. Arina Dähnick, 2018. Courtesy of the artist.

Figure 2. Nora Wendl, 2006, C-print.

Figure 3. Watercolor and graphite on tracing paper, 13" x 25" (33 cm x 63.5 cm), Delineator Edward Duckett, Mies van der Rohe Archive, gift of the architect. © 2024 Artists Rights Society (ARS), New York/VG Bild-Kunst, Bonn.

Figure 4. Edith Farnsworth Residence, Plano, Illinois, c. 1947. Ludwig Mies van der Rohe. Edward A. Duckett Collection, Ryerson and Burnham Art and Architecture Archives, Art Institute of Chicago.

Figure 5. Mary W. "Molly" Dewson, photographer. Courtesy of the Castine Historical Society.

Figure 6. Gerard & Kelly, 2017. Performance view: Farnsworth House, Plano, Illinois, presented by the 2017 Chicago Architecture Biennial. Julia Eichten. Photo: Bradley Glanzrock. Courtesy of the artists and Marian Goodman Gallery. © Adagp Paris, 2024.

Figure 7. Nora Wendl, 2014, C-print.

Figure 8. Nora Wendl, 2015, C-print.

Figure 9. Courtesy of the Newberry Library and Farnsworth family.

Figure 10. Courtesy of Northwestern Memorial Hospital Archives.

Figure 11. Mies van der Rohe retrospective exhibition, Museum of Modern Art, New York, 1947. William Leftwich, photographer. Edward A. Duckett Collection, Ryerson and Burnham Art and Architecture Archives, Art Institute of Chicago.

Figure 12. Gelatin Silver Print. Photographer unknown, undated. Myron Goldsmith fonds, Collection Centre Canadien d'Architecture/Canadian Centre for Architecture, Montréal.

Figure 13. Bruno Taut, Pen and gray ink, and watercolor, preliminary pencil drawing, 1918, on paper from the Gewerbliche Fortbildungsschule (Commercial Further Education School), Bergisch Gladbach, 46 cm x 41.5 cm.

Figure 14. HB-14490-K, Chicago History Museum, Hedrich-Blessing Collection.
Figure 15. Laurence Sarrazin and Nora Wendl, 2014, steel and blown glass.
Figure 16. Photograph by William Dunlap, c. 1951. Courtesy of David W. Dunlap.
Figure 17. Photograph by Edith Farnsworth, c. 1969. Courtesy of the Newberry Library and Farnsworth family.
Figure 18. Nora Wendl, 2018, C-print and trinitite.
Figure 19. Nora Wendl, 2017, C-print.
Figure 20. Nora Wendl, Edith Farnsworth House, 2020.
Figure 21. Nora Wendl, Edith Farnsworth House, 2020.
Figure 22. Nora Wendl, 2021, C-print on fiber rag paper.

Index

45, 103, 118–23, 126–33; rumored relationship with Mies van der Rohe 1, 2, 5–6, 37, 40, 57, 61, 68, 81, 100; séance with, 133–34; as translator, 14–15, 121, 123, 127, 129, 131, 132; violin studies in Italy, 18–19, 26, 64–65; writing on Mies van der Rohe, 8–9; years in Paris, 43–45; "years of vague expansion," 18–19.
—poetry, essays, and collections of poetry translations: "Arsenio," 121; "Artifact," 100; "Boy, Seventeen," 109; Edith Farnsworth Papers at the Newberry Library, 13–19, 58, 61, 119–20, 123; Edith Farnsworth poetry collection at Northwestern Memorial Hospital Archives, 101–4; "February Thaw," 135, 137; "Images of Love," 104; "Is It Time . . . ," 101; "J'accuse," 102; "Night Drifts," 31; *Nu belle fatte: una bella storia,* 129; "The Poet and the Leopards," 103
Farnsworth, Richard, 91, 110, 120
feminism, first-wave American, 42–43
Finfer, June, *The Glass House,* 2, 37
Florence, Italy, 122, 133
Folena, Gianfranco, 130
Forty, Adrian, 96
Fox River, 10, 18, 76, 115, 117–18
Fox River Valley, 155
Freud, Sigmund, 123
Friedman, Alice T., 41
Friedrichstrasse skyscraper project, 8
Furuhashi, Teiji, 83

Gallop, Jane, 12–13
genius, 12, 35, 63, 64, 67–68, 129
Gerard, Brennan, *30*
Gerard, Jim, 101
Gericke, Herbert, 79
Glasraum, 49
glass: as barrier, 3, 22, 24; as obscuring, 3, 39, 68, 105; as reflective, 9, 19, 49, 77, 141; as transparent, 3, 12, 21, 22, 33, 39, 52, 56, 77, 91, 97–99; as utopian material, 74–75
Glass Document II (Wendl), *124*
Glass House (Beth) (Wendl), *36*

Glass House (Projection) (Wendl), *34*
glassblowing, 40–41, 50–51, 79
God: death of (Nietzsche), 6; in perspective drawings, 6; in Mies van der Rohe's architectural philosophy, 7, 88
Goldsmith, Myron, 52, 63, 67–70, *71*
Gordon, Elizabeth, 98
Graff, Rebecca S., 115, 116
Gray, Eileen, 106
Guardini, Romano, 6, 17

Harrington, Kevin, 17, 48
Haskell, Douglas, 76–77
Hathaway, Daniel, 26
Hathaway, Katharine Butler: *The Little Locksmith,* 24–25; in Maine, 24–26, 45; marriage of, 26; in Paris, 26, 43–45
Hedrich, William, 76, *78*
hermeticism, 17
Hitler, Adolf, 19
Ho-Chunk (Wisconsin Winnebago) people, 115
Homer: *The Odyssey,* 127
homophobia, 43, 107
Hopewell people, 114
Hopewell, Mordecai, 144
Hopi people, 112
House Beautiful, 1, 98
Huebner Geering, Jenny, *46, 47*

I Listened (Wendl), *134*
Illinois Institute of Technology (IIT) Campus Master Plan, 23–24
Illini or Illiniwek (Illinois) people, 115
Ireland, 9, 105–7

Jaffe, Michael, 65, 77
Johnson, Philip, 29
Joyce, James, 127

Kkaskaskahamwa (Kaskaskia), 115
Kelly, Ryan, *30*
Kelsky, Karen, 93
Kendall County vs. Mae C. Feeney, Edith B. Farnsworth, et al., 113–17
Kiikaapoi people (Kickapoo), 115

White Sands National Park, 112, 124–26
Willamette River, 62, 74
women: gender stereotypes of, 38, 40, 43, 64, 71, 81, 86, 90, 93, 109; problematic historiography of, 45, 48; in sculpture, 49–50; as symbol, 127–28
World Trade Center Towers, 19
World War I, 42, 74
World War II, 10, 103, 107, 136
Wright brothers, 74

Yamasaki, Minoru: World Trade Center Towers, 19; Wendell O. Pruitt Homes and William Igoe Apartments Complex, 7, 8, 28
Young, Richard, 114

Zamyatin, Yevgeny, 39
Zuni people, 112

NORA WENDL is an essayist, artist, and associate professor of architecture at the University of New Mexico.

The University of Illinois Press
is a founding member of the
Association of University Presses.

———————————————

Composed in 11.5/14 Adobe Garamond Pro
with Gotham display
by Lisa Connery
at the University of Illinois Press
Manufactured by Versa Press, Inc.

University of Illinois Press
1325 South Oak Street
Champaign, IL 61820-6903
www.press.uillinois.edu